NOLO *and* USA TODAY

NOLO
YOUR LEGAL COMPANION

For more than 35 years, Nolo has been helping ordinary folks who want to answer their legal questions, create their own documents, or work with a lawyer more efficiently. Nolo.com provides quick information about wills, house buying, credit repair, starting a business—and just about anything else that's affected by the law. It's packed with free articles, legal updates, resources, and a complete catalog of Nolo books and software.

To find out about any important legal or other changes to this book's contents, sign up for our free update service at Nolo.com/newsletters/index.html, or go to Nolo.com and under "Products," find this book, and click "Legal Updates." And to make sure that you've got the most recent edition of this book, check Nolo's website or give us a call at 800-728-3555.

USA TODAY
The Nation's Newspaper

USA TODAY, the nation's largest circulation newspaper, was founded in 1982. It has nearly 3.9 million readers daily, making it the most widely read newspaper in the country.

USATODAY.com adds blogs, interactive graphics, games, travel resources, and trailblazing network journalism, allowing readers to comment on every story.

Please note

We believe accurate, plain-English legal information should help you solve many of your own legal problems. But this text is not a substitute for personalized advice from a knowledgeable lawyer. If you want the help of a trained professional—and we'll always point out situations in which we think that's a good idea—consult an attorney licensed to practice in your state.

Running a SIDE BUSINESS

How to Create a Second Income

Attorney Richard Stim and Lisa Guerin, J.D.

First Edition	OCTOBER 2009
Editor	ILONA BRAY
Cover Design	JALEH DOANE
Book Design	SUSAN PUTNEY
Proofreading	SUSAN CARLSON GREENE
Index	SONGBIRD INDEXING
Printing	DELTA PRINTING SOLUTIONS, INC.

Stim, Richard.
  Running a side business : how to create a second income / by Rich Stim & Lisa Guerin.
-- 1st ed.
    p. cm.
  ISBN-13: 978-1-4133-1067-2 (pbk.)
  ISBN-10: 1-4133-1067-2 (pbk.)
  1. Supplementary employment. 2. Part-time employment. I. Guerin, Lisa, 1964- II.
Title.
  HD5854.5.S75 2009
  658.4'21--dc22

                        2009021421

Acknowledgments

Thanks to Ilona Bray, Susan Putney, and Janet Portman.

Table of Contents

Your Business Companion

It seems like I've always had a side business. (The earliest one I can remember was an after-school enterprise in which I charted my friends' biorhythms.) It wasn't just the money; there were usually other reasons. Sometimes, I wanted to learn new skills—for example, when I learned how to produce audiobooks. Or, I wanted to exploit and expand existing skills—for example, when I taught night classes for paralegals. Sometimes, I wanted to create something from scratch and to take a shot at the brass ring—like when I began writing children's stories. And when I performed in bands, it was so much fun that I couldn't believe that I also got paid. To paraphrase Will Rogers, I've never met a side business I didn't like.

One reason that side businesses are so likeable is that they're always on the *side*. They don't exist to create a primary source of income. The pressure is off. Side businesses create supplemental income, and, unlike your day job, you call the shots. But the most surprising benefit of a side business is how it affects your mind. It gives you something to think about, something to manage, and something to root for. It's a profitable daydream, a diversion that improves your bottom line.

So, if a side business is so great, why hasn't everyone started one? And why is this the first book devoted totally to creating and running a side business?

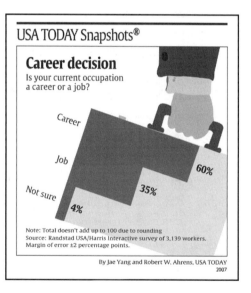

USA TODAY Snapshots®

Career decision
Is your current occupation a career or a job?

Career
Job — 60%
Not sure
35%
4%

Note: Total doesn't add up to 100 due to rounding
Source: Randstad USA/Harris Interactive survey of 3,139 workers.
Margin of error ±2 percentage points.

By Jae Yang and Robert W. Ahrens, USA TODAY
2007

As to the first question, some people just don't want the hassle. Once they finish their 9-to-5, they're happy to put their feet on the ottoman and watch *Desperate Housewives*. Of course, there are also people who want to run a small side business but haven't begun to do it. Their major obstacle is that they don't know how to go about it—for example, they don't know how to choose the right business, how to get started, how to handle money, how to prepare taxes, how to market, or how to deal with contracts. Perhaps they also lack the self-confidence and belief that they can actually do it.

This brings us to our second question: Why hasn't someone written a book about running a side business? One reason could be that most popular business books are written for a strike-it-rich reader. Publishers are eager to preach to the big dreamers but apparently don't think there's a market for those with lower expectations—those who simply want to manage and profit from an enjoyable business diversion.

That's unfortunate. If you're a casual entrepreneur, you deserve a legal and business guide that simplifies and explains all the confusing, challenging, or just plain boring aspects of running a side business.

Good news! You're holding that book.

I can confidently state that this is the best book for anyone interested in running a side business. I believe that my co-author Lisa Guerin and I have created a handbook that will give you all of the confidence, reassurance, and tools you need to keep your side business stable and prosperous.

—Rich Stim

Starting the Right Side Business

A side business is a small enterprise that you run for supplemental income. Side businesses typically augment a 9-to-5 paycheck or bolster retirement savings. Because they're small and personalized, they often provide satisfaction, stimulation, and—if run properly and prudently—long-term revenue and savings.

If you've already started a side business and you're satisfied with your choice, you can skip this chapter. But if you're not sure what type of side business is right for you, or you're wondering if the business you've already started is the best choice, or you're not really sure you're the right person to be running a side business, then read on.

Before You Start: Nine Things to Consider

We wish you could simply spin a wheel to choose the right side business. Because your choice is likely to involve some investment of time and money, it's best to weigh the choices. Here are nine things to consider before starting.

#1: How Will You Make Money?

The bottom line in any side business is ... well, the *bottom line*. This may seem self-evident, but you would be surprised at how many people start businesses without actually knowing how they will make money. If you can't explain to others in one sentence where the money will come from, then you've got a hobby, not a business.

#2: Are You Good at What You Do?

It's not enough to like what you do; you also need to be good at it. Your side business will be most satisfying when your ability and your ambition are closely matched. For example, suppose you want to teach music to youngsters. You may be a great musician, but if you're a poor instructor, you must either improve your teaching skills or consider another side business. You can get better on the job, but you must consider whether you can afford the learning curve.

#3: Are You Experienced?

You'll find it more satisfying (and probably more profitable) to pursue an endeavor in which you have had some experience or at least some exposure. For example, if you've helped your sister at several crafts fairs, you'll have some understanding of the crafts industry and how to sell crafts. This is not to say that you can't gain experience as you proceed (that's axiomatic), but having prior experience can shorten the learning curve.

#4: What's Your Competition?

Before plunging into a new venture, check out the breadth of your competitors and ask yourself if the field is too crowded. Sometimes a crowded field means there is more opportunity (consider the tens of thousands of iPhone apps), but it can also mean no profits (Beanie Babies anyone?). If a field is too crowded, consider whether there is a variation, niche, or alternative. (Hmm, Beanie Baby phone apps?)

#5: Are You Good With People?

Before you choose a side biz, consider the human contact element. Your choice of side business and your level of satisfaction will be directly tied to whether you're a "people person." If you're not good at dealing with kids, for example, then obviously you should forget about working as a children's party clown. The good news is that there are many side businesses—for example, website creation or home cleaning—that require minimal human contact.

#6: What's the Market Demand?

There's a reason why people line up for Apple's new products. Apple understands market demand. If you're unsure whether market demand exists (or whether current demand will continue), don't start that side business. Usually, you can determine the answers with some informal market research. For example, a friend of ours wanted to teach guitar to high school students until he asked around and learned that all the kids wanted to be DJs, not guitar heroes. Sometimes, you can learn enough by informally polling people in your area; in other instances, you may need to use online tools, statistics, or demographics.

#7: Will It Take Over Your Home?

Most side businesses operate out of the home. Before claiming the downstairs bedroom as your eBay shipping and storage center, it's wise to consult with your family or roommates. If space is a concern, you'll have less impact on home life if you maintain a small footprint—for example, a Web designer, freelance writer, or a bookkeeper—or if you work at your clients' location—as does a handyman or an Internet troubleshooter.

#8: Will You Lose Your Job, Family, Money, or Mind?

Keeping it together comes down to how you manage your time. For example, if you run a website that generates ad revenue, do you have the time to monitor Google analytics, tweak your site, and constantly Twitter your customers with new offers? Does your free time sync up with that of your customers—for example, can you install wireless networks *only* during the evenings and weekends? Will you find yourself managing your eBay PowerSeller account at your day job? Can you estimate the hourly needs for your side business before committing to it? For more on this, see the section below, "Can You Really Maintain Your Full-Time Job *and* Your Side Business?"

#9: Sometimes the Best Choice for a Side Business Is None of the Above

Keep in mind that a profit motive, by itself, is usually not enough to sustain a side business. If your sole goal in starting a side business is to feed your bank account, you may be better off with a part-time job. With a job, you won't have to drum up customers, manage your money, take risks, and worry about cash flow. Your decision not to run a side business isn't a reflection on your talent, brains, or perseverance; it's more about your priorities. A side business can take up part (or all) of your free time and, in combination with a full-time job, can be downright exhausting.

Can You Really Maintain Your Full-Time Job *and* Your Side Business?

Here are some things to consider about keeping your full-time job, your side business, and your sanity.

Your employer may not share your enthusiasm for your side business. Your first priority should be to keep things cool with your employer. It's especially important that your employer not perceive your side business as competing in any way. Check your employee handbook in case your company has rules regarding side businesses. Check any other documents you signed when you began working in case you have agreed not to work with anything that conflicts or competes with your employer.

USA TODAY Snapshots®

U.S. job satisfaction declines
Percentage of workers satisfied with their jobs:
61%   59%   51%   52%   47%
1987 1995 2000 2005 2006
Source: The Conference Board, TNS survey of 5,000 U.S. households.
By Jae Yang and Alejandro Gonzalez, USA TODAY 2007

Don't steal office supplies. Don't stock your side business with supplies from your day job. In *The Scorecard at Work* (Holt), author Greg Gutfeld says stealing office supplies is one of the five fastest ways to get fired. You may rationalize this theft by saying "the company can afford it." But since office supplies account for a fairly large chunk of the $67 billion lost to employee theft each year, employers apparently don't think they *can* afford it—and are now more than ever on the lookout for disappearing staplers.

Don't use information from work, including customer lists and trade secrets. Avoid using information you obtain at work for your side business, no matter why you think it's harmless borrowing. Every employer has valuable confidential information that it wants to keep under wraps. It could be a sales plan, a list of customers, a manufacturing process, or a formula for a soft drink. In legal terms, these are your employer's trade secrets. You have an obligation to preserve these secrets, whether or not you signed a nondisclosure agreement.

Don't assume you own what you create for an employer. Even without a written employment agreement, an employer often ends up acquiring ownership of innovations you created in the course of your employment. Tread especially carefully if your side business is based on a product developed during your employment.

Go part-time, flextime, or telecommute. We're mindful that you're reading this book to increase your income, not reduce it. But if you can afford it, consider talking to your employer about: (a) flextime, which lets an employee work a nontraditional schedule—for example, working a full-time job in less than five days; (b) telecommuting, which permits you to work at home some or all of the time; or (c) part-time/job sharing, when two workers share the duties of one full-time job. Don't be dismayed if your employer doesn't offer these options—yet. You may be able to convince your boss to change course. Numerous books, career counselors, and websites

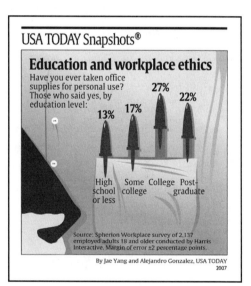

USA TODAY Snapshots®

Education and workplace ethics

Have you ever taken office supplies for personal use? Those who said yes, by education level:

13% 17% 27% 22%

High school or less | Some college | College | Post-graduate

Source: Spherion Workplace survey of 2,137 employed adults 18 and older conducted by Harris Interactive. Margin of error ±2 percentage points.

By Jae Yang and Alejandro Gonzalez, USA TODAY 2007

are devoted to helping you achieve that goal. One site, Work Options (www.workoptions.com), helps you write a proposal for your boss and even provides scripted responses to typical objections.

Get organized. If keeping a job and running your side business is making you feel scattered, take some time to improve your organizational skills. Two of the most popular organizational gurus are David Allen, author of *Getting Things Done* (Penguin), and Julie Morgenstern, author of *Organizing From the Inside Out* (Holt). Fans of David Allen have memorized his mantra, "Do it, delegate it, or defer it." Julie Morgenstern concentrates on organizing your mind first and tasks second. Unless you get your mind in order, she says, you'll continue to create unrealistic schedules that increase frustration.

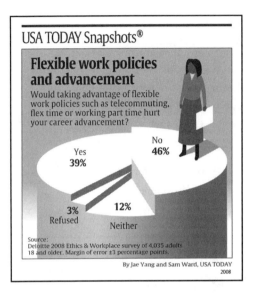

USA TODAY Snapshots®

Flexible work policies and advancement

Would taking advantage of flexible work policies such as telecommuting, flex time or working part time hurt your career advancement?

No
46%

Yes
39%

3%
Refused

12%
Neither

Source:
Deloitte 2008 Ethics & Workplace survey of 4,035 adults 18 and older. Margin of error ±3 percentage points.

By Jae Yang and Sam Ward, USA TODAY
2008

Get help. If you can afford it, sometimes the best way to juggle your job and side business is to bring in someone else to help with your business. You can hire a contractor or employee and pay them based upon sales or other revenue. The point is to find someone to help with the heavy lifting. You may be able to accomplish this without cash payment. Many contractors—particularly in bad economies—are willing to consider bartering. Several websites facilitate long-distance bartering—for example, to exchange online site creation for advertising services. Use terms such as "barter network" or "corporate barter" to locate these services.

Common Side Businesses

Below, we've provided an alphabetical list of some common side businesses. The choices are unlimited—we know someone who sells hand-painted sand dollars—and this list is simply a short survey of popular opportunities. A lot of the information in this section is derived from the *Occupational Outlook Handbook*, available at the Bureau of Labor Statistics (www.bls.gov).

Using a Side Business to "Hedge Your Bets"

Continental Express regional jet pilot Chad Pensiero hopes to fly international routes for a major airline someday. But, unsure he'll ever see that time because of industry turmoil, he's becoming a newspaper publisher on the side.

In October 2004, Pensiero and Jason Foley, a copilot who also works for Continental Express, delivered the first issue of their biweekly, free-distribution shopper. They were already thinking big. Pensiero, who lives in East Stroudsburg, Pennsylvania, hoped to double *The Pocono Classifieds'* first-issue circulation of 10,000 by December and make the paper profitable by the third issue.

"I've always wanted to work for myself," says Pensiero, 30, who has flown for the airline for six years. He says he's confident his own job is secure. But he was driven to start the side business by the general uncertainty in the airline industry.

"I'm senior enough to do OK," he says, "but I've always wanted to fly a 777 into London on a foggy morning, and that may never happen. After September 11, everything changed in the business."

To start the newspaper, Pensiero took voluntary six-month unpaid leave. While that gave him the time he needed, it meant forgoing half his pilot pay of about $60,000 for the year. Pensiero and Foley refinanced their houses and invested their savings in the business, which cost more than $25,000 to start.

Pensiero has no plans to leave aviation. But he says all around him, pilots are hedging their bets, starting new businesses such as selling real estate or taking other sales jobs. "It's pretty common to start a business," he says.

 "Airline workers branch out to make ends meet," by Chris Woodyard, October 21, 2004.

RESOURCE
For a thorough list of inexpensive-to-start side businesses, see *101 Businesses You Can Start, With Less Than One Thousand Dollars: For Stay-at-Home Moms & Dads*, by Heather Shepard (Atlantic).

Adsense and Affiliate Marketing

If you maintain a blog or website, Adsense and Affiliate marketing can be peripheral or primary sources of income for your side business. Both of these marketing businesses place ads on your site and you earn money when someone either clicks the ad (AdSense) or buys the product in the ad (Affiliate marketing)—for example, people click through your site to buy a book at Amazon. (There's much more to these marketing businesses and we provide details in Chapter 2).

 RESOURCE
See *How I Made My First Million on the Internet: And You Can Too*, by Ewen Chia (Morgan James).

Bed and Breakfast

We're hesitant to include B&Bs as a side business—they seem more like a full-time job—but research indicates that many people who run B&Bs do so in addition to a full-time job (or in connection with a spouse who is not working). A bed and breakfast side business must conform to city and state laws, obtain local licenses, abide by local zoning rules (and collect local taxes), and will need to carry commercial liability insurance. You'll have to be a people person, a decent marketer, and willing to enforce the house rules. This is a competitive field affected by general travel trends. According to the Professional Association of Innkeepers International, there are more than 20,000 licensed bed and breakfasts in the United States.

RESOURCE

You can get an idea of your competition and their prices at www.BedandBreakfast.com and www.BBonline.com. See also *How to Open a Financially Successful Bed & Breakfast or Small Hotel*, by Lora Arduser and Douglas R. Brown (Atlantic).

Beauty

Whether you're rendering highlights, creating weaves, providing scalp treatments, sculpturing or repairing nails, providing body waxing, or offering massages, you'll need to look into certification and licensing rules for your state, as well as zoning requirements if clients will come to your home. (Many towns permit home-based beauty businesses with some restrictions.) Also keep in mind that this is a business that is based on health and cleanliness, so a home that is a war zone will not work well as your day spa. If you don't want to operate out of your home, you can always take that blow drier or massage table

to your client's home. Start-up fees are minimal (unless you require expensive salon equipment) and you should look into professional insurance. Extra income can be earned by the sale of hair and beauty products. Managing our nation's hair, nails, and skin is a $21 billion industry.

RESOURCE

See Neil Ducoff's *Fast Forward Salon & Spa Business Resource* (Strategies).

Blogger

A blog is a website at which you write short entries (usually daily) on some subject of interest or expertise. A blog can be a marketing tool— for example, it can attract customers to your consulting business—or it can earn money (or both). Bloggers earn money either directly from advertising, sponsorship, and affiliate commissions or from book deals, licensing, or salary (yes, some people are paid to write blogs). Setup fees are minimal and many services are free, for example, www.blogger.com. According to the *Wall Street Journal*, there are over 1.7 million people earning money from blogs in the United States, and approximately 450,000 claim to be making a full-time living. (There's more about blogs in Chapter 2.)

> **RESOURCE**
> See Darren Rowse's ProBlogger site (www.problogger.com), or read his book, *ProBlogger: Secrets for Blogging Your Way to a Six-Figure Income* (Wiley).

Catering and Food Preparation

Off-premises catering—serving food away from your home or kitchen —is a rapidly growing industry and profitable (profit margins are usually 20% or higher). Whether you act as a personal chef or party caterer, you'll need to learn about state and local certification and licensing, as well as zoning requirements. You'll need to decide whether to use your own kitchen at home, or whether you'll prepare food on-site at the client's location. Start-up costs are minimal—usually between $500 and $1,000. Some caterers lacking start-up funds save money by initially renting supplies (dishes, silverware, and so on) until they can afford to own them. Obviously, cooking skills are essential, but equally important are skills in management (you may have to hire temp workers), planning (what time does that soufflé come out?), and marketing (you'll definitely need to be a people person).

> **RESOURCE**
> See Denise Vivaldo's *How to Start a Home-Based Catering Business* (Home-Based Business Series).

Child Care

Taking care of the little ones is a timeless, low-tech business. If it's accomplished at the client's home, the start-up costs are minimal, if any. If you're planning to run a day-care center, however, things become more complicated (you'll encounter local and state certification and licensing) and more expensive (such as toys, juice boxes, and insurance). As women continue to move into the workforce, the need for child care increases, making this one of the fastest-growing businesses in the United States (over $11 billion annually) with expected growth of over 40% in coming years.

> **RESOURCE**
> See *How to Open & Operate a Financially Successful Child Care Service*, by Tina Musial (Atlantic).

Cleaning and Janitorial

A cleaning service typically cleans homes; a janitorial service cleans offices. Cleaning is a side business that will never go out of fashion and will almost always generate a good profit margin (over $100 billion of revenue generated annually in the United States). What's interesting about the industry is that because it is so low tech and labor intensive, it is populated by thousands of sole proprietorships. Start-up costs are low and customers usually come from word of mouth.

> **RESOURCE**
> See Beth Morrow's *How to Open & Operate a Financially Successful Cleaning Service* (Atlantic).

Consultant

Consultants—we're referring to any expert from an accountant to a tutor—commonly work out of a home office, don't have employees, and, thanks to modern technology, can set up their businesses with the aid of a computer, Internet access, and a telephone. The three challenges common to all consulting businesses are: (1) finding clients, (2) pricing properly, whether billing at an hourly or project rate, and (3) acquiring and maintaining your expertise.

 RESOURCE
See Alan Weiss's *Getting Started in Consulting* (Wiley).

Craftsperson

No longer limited to crafts fairs and farmers' markets, handmade crafts can be found in malls, mainline retail outlets, and online shops (check out www.etsy.com). Since many craftspeople start their trades as hobbies and then find a market for their goods, the start-up costs are low (you already own that leather punch). Factor in additional costs for studio rentals or for exhibition fees at shows. Profit margins vary dramatically, depending on whether you're selling direct or on consignment (consignees usually take 25% to 50%).

 RESOURCE
See *Craft, Inc.,* by Meg Mateo Ilasco (Chronicle).

eBay/Amazon

According to one report, 700,000 people in the United States rely on eBay as a secondary (or primary) source of income, and 14% of eBay sellers report that they retired from their days jobs to work full-time on eBay. Lately, many eBay sellers are expanding or moving their operations to Amazon.com—in 2008, *The New York Times* reported that for the first time, more Americans clicked over to Amazon than to eBay—where the reselling business is focused on fixed prices, not auctions. The start-up requirements for an eBay or Amazon enterprise include a computer and high-speed Internet connection, a credit card and PayPal account, and of course, something to sell. It's that last item that creates the greatest challenge—especially once you've cleared out your basement or garage. (There's more on this side business in Chapter 2.)

RESOURCE
See *The eBay Business Start-Up Kit*, by Richard Stim (Nolo), and *Amazon Top Seller Secrets*, by Brad Schepp and Debra Schepp (Amacom).

Gardener or Landscaper

Ahh … the great outdoors. Here's a side business for those with a green thumb and weed whacker. Marketing is usually simple—your work serves as a public calling card and revenues are generated from word of mouth. Billings are either by the hour or by the project (compare competitor's prices at craigslist. com). Start-up costs are usually minimal (you may even be able to use a client's tools) and there are no special certification requirements.

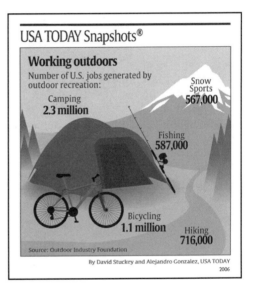

USA TODAY Snapshots®

Working outdoors
Number of U.S. jobs generated by outdoor recreation:

Camping
2.3 million

Snow Sports
567,000

Fishing
587,000

Bicycling
1.1 million

Hiking
716,000

Source: Outdoor Industry Foundation

By David Stuckey and Alejandro Gonzalez, USA TODAY
2006

RESOURCE
See Owen Dell's *How to Start a Home-Based Landscaping Business* (Home-Based Business).

Graphic Artist/Designer

Graphic designers create visual solutions using color, type, illustration, photography, animation, and various print and layout techniques.

You don't need to be Michelangelo to make money as a graphic artist; the United States has more than 250,000 full-time graphic artists and 25% are self-employed. A successful graphic artist needs to be willing to work with oft-opinionated clients. (The biggest challenge for many artists is to sublimate personal tastes in order to please the client.) This is a competitive field in which marketing and people skills often make the difference. Start-up expenses vary depending on the type of work performed, and you'll need a high-end computer workstation and graphics software that can often be expensive.

RESOURCE
See the Graphics Artist's Guild (GAG) website (www.gag.org).

Home Health Care

The home health care industry is expected to grow by more than 50% in coming years as the U.S. demographic ages—more than 80 million people are hitting senior status. Currently, more than seven million people receive home health care services, making it a $45 billion industry. About one out of three home care aides works part-time; most aides work with a number of different clients, each job lasting a few hours, days, or weeks. Start-up costs vary, as do certification and licensing requirements, depending on the tasks performed and state and local laws.

RESOURCE
See *Home Health Care Provider: A Guide to Essential Skills,* by Emily Prieto (Springer).

Home Repair and Installation (Services)

Most contractors prefer major remodels over smaller one-off jobs. That factor—combined with an aging demographic, the lack of leisure time for do-it-yourselfers, and more complicated repairs—leaves a wide-open market for anyone knowledgeable about carpentry, plumbing, electrical, or installations (especially alarms and solar panels).

RESOURCE
See *The Handyman Business Guide to Success,* by Bob Cheal (CreateSpace).

Musician

Making music is an ideal side business because the hours required—usually nights and weekends—rarely interfere with a 9-to-5. (If some lout yells, "Don't quit your day job," at your next show, tell him that you don't need to; there's no time conflict.) You may be surprised to learn that 35% of the money-making gigs for musicians are for religious organizations (the fastest-growing area of work for musicians), and 11% involve work for small community or chamber groups.

RESOURCE
See *Music Law,* by Richard Stim (Nolo).

Personal Assistant/Concierge

Since personal assistants are often on call 24/7, we were hesitant to include this in a survey of side businesses. However, we are informed that some personal assistants (or PAs) are needed only for specific personal tasks, which often can be performed during off hours. The fact is that many regular folks, overwhelmed by their multitasking schedules, are hiring others to help with shopping, taking the kids to school, or standing in line at the post office. In addition, there's a growing business for people who provide concierge services, usually over the Internet, helping others with purchases, appointments, and travel arrangements. Start-up costs are minimal (a virtual concierge will need a dedicated phone line, high-speed Internet, and a computer) and people skills are essential.

RESOURCE
See *The Two-Second Commute,* by Christine Durst (Career Press).

Personal Trainer/Fitness Instructor

This broad category includes everything from nutrition and weight consultants to yoga and Pilates instructors (and don't forget those post-natal exercise specialists, too). The personal trainer business is booming (expect a 50% growth over the next decade). Start-up costs are low (certification costs—a key component in this business—will run from $250 to $600). To succeed you'll need strong people skills and an ability to market yourself. You'll also have to decide if you want to operate as a freelancer or work out of a fitness center.

> **RESOURCE**
> See Starting a Personal Training Business (www.starting-a-personal-training-business.com), where you can find a comparison chart of the various certification programs. For more on certification, see the American Council on Exercise, the Aerobics and Fitness Association of America, the American Fitness Professionals and Associates, the National Federation of Professional Trainers, or the International Fitness Professionals Association. Many of these offer home study courses.

Pets

Our furry friends are pampered; in the past two decades, the amount spent on them has doubled. Whether you walk them, groom them, train them, house-sit them, or create pet parties (Pupperware, anyone?), there's a pet side business for you. Start-up costs vary from minimal (several leashes and a pooper scooper for dog walkers) to substantial. (Will your neighbors share your enthusiasm for your fantasy-themed doggie hotel?)

> **RESOURCE**
> See 101 Best Businesses for Pet Lovers, by Joseph Nigro and Nicholas Nigro (Sphinx) or How To Open & Operate a Financially Successful Pet Sitting Business, by Angela W. Duea (Atlantic).

Photographer

As with musicians, the combination of the Internet and digital technol-ogy has drastically altered the business landscape for photographers. On the one hand, it's much easier for photographers to sell and license their wares via websites such as Shutterstock (www.shutterstock.com) and iStockphoto (www.istockphoto.com). On the other hand, there is far more competition and the payment—sometimes as low as a $1 per use at iStockphoto—makes it harder to earn a substantial profit. Others may find a bigger profit margin and more reliable income as an event photographer (think weddings, amateur sports events, and reunions) or portrait photographer.

> **RESOURCE**
> See *The Photographer's Survival Guide: How to Build and Grow a Successful Business,* by Amanda Sosa Stone and Suzanne Sease (Amphoto).

Programmer/Web Developer/App Developer

If you're gifted with programming skills—and, in particular, if you can combine those skills with some other talent such as graphic design—then you may be able to run a successful side business as a coder, website designer, or applications developer. Coders can do freelance work for others or independently develop programs that can be offered for sale online. As for creating independent programs for sale, many coders have participated in the gold rush of apps and widgets—small software applications that are installed on computers, phones, and iPods. (In one famous get-rich-quick story, a developer earned $20,000 a day from sales of his iPhone app.)

> **RESOURCE**
> See Rent a Coder (www.rentacoder.com), which makes it easy for you to submit bids on existing jobs. See also Stephen Fishman's *Legal Guide to Web & Software Development* (Nolo).

Steer Clear of an Illegal Side Business

When the pay from his day job proved to be insufficient, one employee of the TSA (Transportation Security Agency) decided to start his own side business, selling drugs to customers from his "home" and at the airport. The side business (and his TSA job) came to a crashing halt in 2009 when, alas, the drugs hit the fan—so to speak.

If you're running an illegal side business, which is any business that offers a product or service that violates the law, you'll have a unique set of problems for which we can't offer much assistance (except to remind you that you have the right to remain silent). Even a clever illegal enterprise can get tripped up by that oldest of professionals, the tax collector. Failing to report income from an illegal enterprise is what caused the notorious Al Capone to tumble from his perch. (Resource: *The Criminal Law Handbook*, by Paul Bergman and Sara Berman (Nolo).)

Property Management and Rental

Whether you're managing property for someone else, or renting out property that you own, you'll need some expertise in a variety of areas in order to manage this side business lawfully and safely. For example, you'll need to understand tax rules regarding rentals, know how to screen and choose tenants, handle the legal end of leases and evictions, and deal with problem tenants.

RESOURCE
See *First-Time Landlord: Renting Out a Single-Family Home*, by Janet Portman, Marcia Stewart, and Michael Molinski (Nolo).

Telemarketer/Salesperson

A typical telemarketing/sales position involves selling goods or services, such as magazine subscriptions, usually over the phone. In some cases, it may involve meeting with customers in person or soliciting donations for a nonprofit organization. Setup is minimal: Usually, all you need is a dedicated phone line. The pay is usually structured as an hourly base rate—$6 to $49 an hour—plus a commission for every good or service sold or appointment scheduled.

> **RESOURCE**
> See job boards Monster.com and CareerBuilder.com. Run keyword searches for "telemarketer" or "telesales." Or check out companies that hire home-based telemarketers such as TeleReach, Intrep, and West Corporation.

Do You Need a Business Plan?

In his book *Burn Your Business Plan*, author David Gumpert argues that business plans are a bunch of mumbo jumbo with crazy projections. Moreover, he says that investors and bankers routinely disregard them because they really only want to see one thing: evidence of demand for your products and services. For purposes of your side business, we tend to agree. Preparing a full-blown business plan would be overkill for someone who teaches clarinet, creates handmade mailboxes, jams every weekend as a wedding DJ, writes a blog, or sells handmade rugs.

That said, some people have big plans for their side businesses. They want them to grow and prosper and they may eventually seek investment or loans. The business world still finds something comforting about that stack of papers marked "business plan" and routinely requests them when you put your hand out. More importantly, some elements of a business plan can benefit every side business owner—for example, the ability to predict cash flow.

If you're interested in preparing a business plan, don't worry. As with everything else in small business management, you can find people and products that can simplify the business plan process. Start by looking at business plans for businesses similar to yours. Many, many plans are available online. Start at Bplans.com, where over 60 sample plans created with *Business Plan Pro* software are posted. Once you've got an idea of what your plan should look like, map out your own using do-it-yourself products or by hiring someone to help you. Expect to pay $200 to $1,000 for professional help.

RESOURCE
See *How to Write a Business Plan*, by Mike McKeever (Nolo); or *Business Plan Pro*, business-plan-creation software from Palo Alto Software.

Avoid Side-Business Scams

You may be inclined to start a side business after seeing ads that make big promises: They typically describe a paradise in which you make thousands of dollars a month (despite your lack of experience) while setting your own hours and working as much or as little as you wish. All you have to do to is purchase start-up materials and training, an up-front investment the advertisers imply you'll earn back many times over! Chances are you won't fall for this ad, right? Let's hope not. Just in case, we've summarized a few of the more popular scams (excerpted from the Nolo book, *The Work From Home Handbook: Flex Your Time, Improve Your Life*, by attorneys Stephen Fishman and Diana Fitzpatrick).

Medical Claims Processing Scams

The scam promises to train you in medical transcription or medical coding (matching up medical procedures with the appropriate insurance codes). You're promised a database of physician contacts and everything you need to start a service from home, all for a several-hundred-dollar fee. What you get for your money is usually some outdated or inappropriate software and a list of local physician contacts that may have been photocopied from the yellow pages. Your chances of earning money with these materials? Zero.

Product Assembly Scams

This scheme works by asking you to purchase the materials and instructions for putting together products like baby booties, plastic signs, or toy clowns. You're told that a company has already committed to purchase the assembled products at a significant profit to you, provided you follow the instructions and meet quality standards. But once you submit your assembled products for sale, you're invariably told that they don't meet "quality standards." You'll get nothing in return for your investment and time but some unsellable merchandise.

Envelope-Stuffing Scams

A company promises—maybe even "guarantees"—hundreds of dollars a week, just for stuffing envelopes in your own home. The ads appeal to many people because no training is necessary and you can do it while watching *Oprah*. The reality is

USA TODAY Snapshots®

Different age groups and different goals
Percentage of age group ranking these aspects of career development as most important:
- ■ Learning new skills
- ▨ Pay increases
- ▨ Career path

18 to 26: 31%, 22%, 21%
27 to 41: 27%, 31%, 33%
42 to 61: 19%, 14%, 8%

Source: Randstad USA survey of 2,906 adults 18 and older conducted by Harris Interactive. Margin of error ±2 percentage points.

By Jae Yang and Suzy Parker, USA TODAY 2006

that no established business actually depends on at-home workers to stuff its envelopes anymore—it's a highly mechanized operation using sophisticated mass-mailing techniques and equipment. When you respond to an ad for at-home envelope stuffing (usually by paying a fee), you don't get envelopes to stuff. Instead, you receive promotional material on other work-at-home programs.

Direct Sales Pyramid Schemes

Unfortunately, a fair number of crooks have taken the direct-sales model —popularized by Avon and Tupperware—and corrupted it into a work-from-home ploy commonly known as a "pyramid scheme." In these schemes, companies earn money primarily by recruiting new investors to purchase large quantities of product for resale. There is usually no real market for the products, and the company puts no effort into product advertising or marketing. The more "sales representatives" who sign up, the more money the people at the top earn, regardless of the number of products actually sold to consumers. Sooner or later, the pyramid collapses.

Recognizing Other Work-at-Home Scams

Here are some things to remember about side-business scams:

- Be wary of any opportunity that promises you'll earn thousands of dollars a month or more.
- Watch out for the "no experience necessary" line, which is used to reel in the most vulnerable side-business workers.
- Be suspicious of any company you've never heard of.
- Avoid opportunities that require you to pay cash before you get started.
- Ask for references. Don't settle for written testimonials, which are easy to fabricate.

What If ... ? Should You Consider Quitting Your Day Job?

There are many reasons to keep your day job. It's your primary source of income and it may be hard, if not impossible to get a new job. Your regular job provides a sense of security—and then there are the employment benefits, assuming you're lucky enough to get health insurance, dental insurance, stock options, vacation days, pension plans, or discounts at Six Flags.

Leaving your day job can also affect your credit rating—having a 9-to-5 makes it easier to borrow money and get credit cards and loans. The day job also provides a valuable tax benefit, because at tax time, your dual identity lets you deduct your business losses from your day job income.

From Realtor to Jeweler:
How a Side Business Can Provide a Safety Net

Ramona Garcia, 38, of Corona, California, considers herself one of the lucky ones. She and her husband were Realtors. After the housing market collapsed, she forged a new career selling jewelry through a direct-sales business called Silpada Designs. She took a risk when times were tight and decided to buy a starter kit and some jewelry to sell and began planning parties of friends and neighbors to display the jewelry and try to drum up sales.

It was nerve-racking at first. But she says her business experience and the determination she developed as a Realtor allowed her to turn a side business into a prosperous new career that now helps support her family.

"I consider it a blessing," Garcia says.

Not only that, she says she enjoys the work far more than being a Realtor, which meant having to always make herself available for clients. Throwing jewelry parties, she says, is fun and has renewed her confidence. Her husband found a job as a site-acquisition rep for cellphone companies.

"I love my job, and I didn't love real estate," Garcia says. "Real estate was very stressful. The phone would ring up to midnight. I was always on pins and needles."

Yet the experience, in the long run, turned into an advantage. "Being a Realtor for ten years and being that responsible for big things in people's lives—it creates a business background. Return phone calls on time. Don't flake out. This is a fun job compared to a necessary job."

 "Realtors live close to the edge; Some who sold homes now fear losing them," by Stephanie Armour, August 7, 2008.

Of course, if you're not obligated to support anyone, indifferent to your current day job, flush with cash, in love with your side business, and not in need of discount employee tickets to your local hockey team, you may be an ideal candidate for quitting your day job and expanding your side business.

USA TODAY Snapshots®

Finding a new job
Would it be easy or difficult for the average worker who was laid off from his/her job to find a similar job at the same pay?

Difficult 76%

Easy 22%

Don't know 2%

Source: The Career Confidence Index survey of 1,001 full-time workers conducted by Right Management in September 2006. Margin of error ±4 percentage points.

By Jae Yang and Dave Merrill, USA TODAY
2007

Before you take the big step, be sure there's firm footing where you will land. We advise that you do some basic financial forecasting. Estimate living expenses for a year by making a budget based on the past year (or past two years, if possible). Will you have enough income from your business to live and pay your expenses (including health insurance)? Do you have a financial cushion like a savings account that will pay all expenses for six months? How close are you to retirement age, and how will leaving your job affect your retirement? There are no bright lines for determining the right financial mix, but when you weigh these factors you should feel comfortable that you could weather a worst-case scenario.

You also need to consider the psychological impact. How much of your identity is embedded in your current day job? What are you going to miss about it? Many departing employees are surprised by how much they miss the social life provided by a regular job. How does your family feel? Will they support your decision? Are people counting on you to take care of them? There are no simple yes or no answers. You need to examine all of these personal factors before making your decision. Experts use self-actualization techniques to help you make these decisions. You can see how these techniques work in Barbara Sher's book, *I Could Do Anything If I Only Knew What It Was* (Dell).

If you do decide to quit, don't burn your bridges—you may want the job back. And before you leave your job, schedule any last doctor and dental appointments.

As you consider your options, be sure not to violate noncompetition and nonsolicitation agreements. A noncompetition agreement (also known as a noncompete or a covenant not to compete) is a contract in which you agree not to compete with your former employer for a period of time. A nonsolicitation agreement restricts your ability to solicit your former employer's clients or employees. These two agreements are often folded into an employment agreement or become part of a termination agreement that an employee must sign to get a severance package. If your side business is competitive, you'll likely be in violation of the noncompete and your employer will be able to shut it down.

USA TODAY Snapshots®

Trading places

Do you think you could do as good a job or better than your boss does if you switched positions for a day?

Yes 43%

No 25%

Not sure 33%

Source:
Yahoo HotJobs survey of 1,271 employees.
Margin of error ±3 percentage points.

By Jae Yang and Sam Ward, USA TODAY
2008

If You Go Online

n a famous *New Yorker* cartoon, one canine in front of a computer tells another by his side, "On the Internet, nobody knows you're a dog." On the Internet, nobody knows you're a side business. The Web provides the opportunity for a side business owner (at home in her pajamas) to present a product line that appears as competitive and inviting as its big-business cousins. At the same time, the Internet allows your cleaning or child care business to communicate with existing customers—perhaps providing access to a scheduling calendar—and to send out information that sells your services to potential customers.

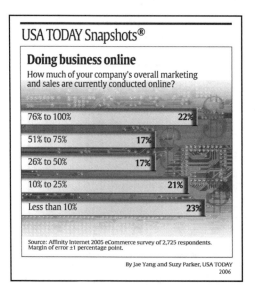

USA TODAY Snapshots®

Doing business online

How much of your company's overall marketing and sales are currently conducted online?

76% to 100% — 22%

51% to 75% — 17%

26% to 50% — 17%

10% to 25% — 21%

Less than 10% — 23%

Source: Affinity Internet 2005 eCommerce survey of 2,725 respondents. Margin of error ±1 percentage point.

By Jae Yang and Suzy Parker, USA TODAY 2006

Whether your new side business operates solely on the Internet or just has some Web-based component—for example, a jewelry maker who also sells on eBay—you'll find that you'll need and benefit from some knowledge about going online. For experienced Internet business owners, this chapter may seem too elementary; for those without any experience, it may seem too technical. We extend apologies to both. We're trying to provide a middle ground, basic enough not to scare away newbies, and detailed enough to be informative. In this chapter, we'll show you how to:

- get lots of cool stuff for free
- invoice customers and get paid using online payment systems
- sell stuff via Amazon or eBay
- earn money using Google Adsense and affiliate accounts
- learn the (very) basics of driving visitors, or traffic to a site
- set up a website in 24 hours, and
- understand the basic legal rules for operating online.

If you're staying away from the Internet out of fear (you're afraid of computers and don't know how to use Google), confusion (you know a little bit, but the whole thing seems overwhelming), or a concern for costs (you're pretty sure you can't afford it, whatever it is), then check out this chapter. You'll be surprised at how much you can manage on your own. And remember, having a high IQ is not a requirement for traveling into cyberspace (as you'll soon become aware once you begin receiving junk emails).

You Don't Have to Drink the Kool-Aid

Despite what we say above (and what your friends may say as well), you can operate a successful side business without buying a computer or connecting to the Internet. That's right! You can be perfectly happy without a website, blog, or even an online presence. Many businesses rely solely on a telephone and an answering machine (and word-of-mouth marketing). Bottom line: If you're satisfied with the way your side business is marketed and you already have more business than you can handle, you probably don't need to establish a presence in cyberspace (although you might want to consider an email account, as explained below).

Free Stuff

Many small business owners are unaware of the great free stuff that's available on the Web. (And, no, we're not talking about illegal downloads of *The Matrix* or Kelly Clarkson MP3s.) Many business and personal services are offered gratis, and the number of such services seems to be increasing as online entrepreneurs realize that giving some things away for free is a great way to sell other stuff. Consider this scenario: You set up a free blog to describe home repair tips. You include—at no charge to you—Google Adsense, which peppers your blog with ads for hardware supplies. Users are attracted to your tips, they click on the ads, and each time they do so, pennies drop into your Google account. Talk about low start-up costs! (Of course, it's not always so easy, as we'll describe below.) Here's an idea of some of the free stuff that can help your side business.

Free Email

For the less than 2% of readers who don't have an email account, here's some good news. You don't need to own a computer to get an email account and you don't even need an Internet connection. If you have access to a public computer at a library or Internet café, you can create a free email account in minutes. If you don't know how, ask someone to show you how to get on the Internet (it usually involves two or three clicks), then go to any of the free email websites—Gmail, Yahoo, Hotmail—and set up an account. (If you've never used a computer mouse, you may need an explanation.) You can track your email on your cell phone, smartphone, and a variety of other handheld devices (although there may be a usage fee).

> **RESOURCE**
> Hotmail (www.hotmail.com), Gmail (www.gmail.com), and Yahoo (www.yahoo.com) are three popular free email sources.

Free Blogs

A blog (short for Web log) is the fastest way to acquire Internet real estate. Initially, blogs were used as journals. Nowadays, they've come to mean any frequently and easily updated Web page. A blog provides a way for people to learn about your business or may even *be* your business if you rely on a click-through program like Adsense or Amazon Affiliates (described in more detail, below). Check it out; it really is very simple. You can list contact information, provide a bio, and post regularly updated information about your business. For example, check out the Crixa Cakes blog-styled site, www.crixa.net (hmmm!). Daily postings include specials of the day as well as job postings and other information. The advantage of a blog is that you can establish one in less than an hour. The disadvantage is that in order to maintain the public's interest, you'll need to regularly refresh it with new information. And if you're *really* serious about making money from your blog and driving traffic to it, you may eventually have to liberate it from the free blogging site and set up your own site (more on that later).

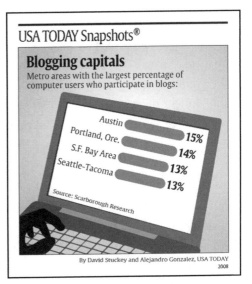

USA TODAY Snapshots®

Blogging capitals
Metro areas with the largest percentage of computer users who participate in blogs:

Austin —
Portland, Ore. — **15%**
S.F. Bay Area — **14%**
Seattle-Tacoma — **13%**
13%

Source: Scarborough Research

By David Stuckey and Alejandro Gonzalez, USA TODAY
2008

RESOURCE
Three free resources for setting up a blog are Blogger (www.blogger.com), Typepad (www.typepad.com), or WordPress (www.wordpress.com). Information on creating a successful blog can be found at ProBlogger (www.problogger.com).

Free Online Calendars, Spreadsheets, Photo Storage, and Documents

Welcome to the "cloud." In tech parlance, cloud computing is when your services are provided and stored online. Instead of searching for that document, photo, or calendar on your work computer or your home computer, you can store it in the cloud—that is, cyberspace. To see how it works, sign up for a Gmail account, sign in, and click one of the links in the upper-left-hand corner (calendar, documents, or photos).

These links give you free word processing software and document storage, free spreadsheet software and storage, free photo galleries, and a free calendar. All of these tools may help you in managing your side business and they may have an extra benefit in that you can provide limited public access to them to your customers or clients. So if, for example, you'd like clients to schedule appointments, you can have them access your free calendar to see what's available. Want customers to see examples of the sweaters you knit? Post pictures on your free photo gallery.

RESOURCE
See Gmail (www.gmail.com); Zoho (which has free and paid platforms), (www.zoho.com); and ThinkFree (which offers some free and some paid services), (www.thinkfree.com). Although it doesn't offer online services, OpenOffice.org offers a free suite of downloadable office software similar to Microsoft *Office* (www.openoffice.org).

Free Surveys

If you're looking for customer feedback or you're doing some market research, sites such as Survey Monkey allow you to do it for free.

RESOURCE
See Survey Monkey (www.surveymonkey.com).

Free To-Do Lists

Keeping track of your to-do list is tricky when you've got multiple lists living on your work computer, home computer, smartphone, and iPod. Sites such as Doris and Toodledo manage your lists for you by keeping the main list online and syncing them to smaller applications widgets that live on your personal devices.

RESOURCE
See Doris (www.dorisapp.com) and Toodledo (www.toodledo. com).

Free Faxes

Say goodbye to that clunky fax machine and instead embrace free online fax services. You upload documents and provide the fax number and these sites deliver, usually with a paid ad on your cover sheet. If you want the ad-free version there's usually a fee of $1 or $2 per fax.

RESOURCE
See Faxzero (www.faxzero.com), and Freefax (www.freefax.com).

Free Websites

Let's say you run a mobile hair salon and you just want a site that provides some basic information, a biography, a synopsis of your services, and perhaps some useful material for customers, like tips on hair maintenance or photos of some of your most popular cuts. You can use one of the many free offerings—for example, Google Sites—which make it easy to create a professional-looking website. The disadvantage is that your site may look slightly generic (since you'll choose from a limited number of templates) and your domain name (your address on the Web) will be more complicated than most. At Google Sites, for example, your address would be http://sites.google.com/site/mobilehairsalon (instead of www.mobilehairsalon.com if you created a paid site as described below).

RESOURCE
See Google Sites (www.sites.google.com), Yola (www.yola.com), Webs (www.webs.com), Wetpaint (www.wetpaint.com), and Weebly (www.weebly.com).

Invoice Customers and Get Paid Online

PayPal (www.paypal.com) is an automated online payment system that enables anyone with an email address to make payments from across the country or around the world. Because the system works so well, and because it also enables the use of credit cards (as part of its Merchant Services), PayPal has become a premier payment system for small business owners. Sending money via PayPal is free, but receiving money may be subject to a fee depending on the type of PayPal account you have. In other words, if you're selling stuff online, PayPal offers a simple way to accept payments without establishing a credit card merchant account (and dealing with the associated fees and expenses).

But wait there's more! PayPal isn't just for those who sell goods. The system also allows anyone—including service providers—to create invoices that enable your customers (even those who know nothing about PayPal) to use the system. You can create invoices in several ways:

- **Email.** Create an email invoice by filling out PayPal's online invoice form.

- **Request Money.** Use PayPal's "Request Money" page to send a customer an invoice directly from PayPal.

- **Quickbooks.** Use the Payment Request Wizard for *Quickbooks*, which enables you to create an invoice from within your *Quickbooks* program.

- **Outlook.** Use the Payment Request Wizard for *Outlook*, which enables you to create an invoice from within your Microsoft *Outlook* email program.

Some alternatives to PayPal include:

- **Google Checkout.** Another alternative to establishing an online credit card merchant account is to create a Google Checkout Merchant Account. Google Checkout is primarily for the sale of tangible and digital (downloadable) goods, although it can also be used to process transactions for services and subscriptions. Like PayPal, Google Checkout accepts major credit and debit cards, including VISA, MasterCard, American Express, and Discover. Buyers enter their credit or debit card information when they first sign up for Google Checkout and can select their preferred payment type during checkout.

- **Checkout by Amazon**. Amazon bills this as a "complete e-commerce checkout solution." Using the Amazon Checkout system, customers at your website get the same checkout experience as they would at Amazon, including Amazon's 1-Click tools.

RESOURCE
See PayPal (www.paypal.com), Google Checkout (www.checkout.google.com), and Checkout by Amazon (www.payments.amazon.com).

Are You an Expert?

Here's an online side business you might not have considered. If you have specialized knowledge in an area—for example, you're an expert on G.I. Joe action figures—and you enjoy sharing that knowledge with others, you might want to consider a position as a home-based online expert for a website such as About.com, Just Answer, or ChaCha. At About.com, you can earn a minimum of $500 per month for writing articles on your area of expertise. At other sites, you may be paid per question, usually $2 to $10. There are minimal setup costs—a home computer and high-speed Internet access.

Sell Stuff via Amazon or eBay

If you've got a computer, Internet connection, packing material, a PayPal account, and some stuff to sell, you can begin selling on eBay or Amazon right now.

eBay

To start selling on eBay, you need to register. It's free (you must be over 18 and have a valid email address), and you must obtain a seller's account (you'll need a credit card). eBay has several formats for listing items for sale but the vast majority of transactions are completed by means of a Standard Auction listing. These are auctions that are open for fixed time periods—typically five to seven days—and the highest bidder at the end of that time period purchases the merchandise. Merchandise can also be sold at a fixed price with a Buy It Now designation. (You cannot sell everything on eBay. Some items are restricted, such as alcohol, firearms, lock-picking equipment, and body parts—yes, it has been tried.)

Every eBay member has a private My eBay page, which tracks recent transactions and advises you when action is needed—for example, when you need to provide feedback or respond to a seller inquiry. Consider the My eBay page a basic auction management tool.

eBay Motors. eBay Motors is the number one automotive site on the Internet. It's estimated that 40% of the time consumers spend looking for cars online is spent at eBay Motors. There you'll find every type of vehicle and automotive part from sedans to jet skis to motorcycles to SUVs to RVs. Best of all, eBay Motors combines unique research features and protection plans with eBay's popular listing tools. The rules for selling and buying at eBay Motors are basically the same as for regular auction items.

Amazon

Like eBay, Amazon offers a few methods for you to use in selling. The basic program is referred to as Selling on Amazon, and using it, you can sell goods in any of the myriad categories seen at the world's largest online store. (You'll need prior approval to sell some goods such as cell phones, jewelry, personal computers, shoes, and apparel.) If you are looking to sell only a few products or expect to have fewer than 40 orders a month, you can sell your items as an individual for a per-product closing fee of $0.99. If you sell more than 40 items per month, you'll need a Pro Merchant account ($39.99 per month). Posting items is very simple. Simply search for the item on Amazon.com and click the Sell Yours Here button. For example, if you've got a used CD of *The Best of King Curtis*, you would find the item at Amazon, click the button to sell yours, and *voilà*. (Make sure you have the correct product; one title can have several editions or formats.) If someone purchases your item, you'll get an email notification. The buyer pays instantly. Amazon pays you after deducting fees. There are other choices at Amazon as well, including Webstores (which we discuss below) and the Advantage Program, by which an

USA TODAY Snapshots®

Shopping at small online businesses

Three out of four respondents are likely to shop at small online businesses such as boutique, niche or specialty stores for unusual or hard-to-find items. Top incentives to shop online:

90% Free shipping
69% Online discounts
64% No-hassle return policy
24% Gift certificates

Note: Multiple responses allowed
Source: Yahoo Small Business/Harris Interactive survey of 2,766 online adults 18 and older. Margin of error: ±3 percentage points.

By Jae Yang and Karl Gelles, USA TODAY
2007

artist, author, or publisher with book, music, video, or DVD titles to sell can place them in the Amazon.com catalog and have Amazon handle the orders.

eBay Stores vs. Amazon Webstores

eBay stores and Amazon Webstores are basically a series of Web pages that showcase your inventory and cross-promote your sales, at eBay auctions or at Amazon store pages. These stores are easy to create, easy to use, and make receiving payments from customers a simple process.

eBay Stores. Selling via an eBay store offers a longer selling period (either 30 days or "Good 'Til Cancelled") than an online eBay auction. Also, the listing fees and Final Value fees for selling fixed-price eBay store items are generally lower than if they were sold at auction. The Good Til Cancelled feature is especially helpful because you don't need to constantly relist unsold items. The disadvantages of an eBay store are the monthly expenses ($15.95 for a Basic Store, $49.95 for a Premium Store) and that store sales will not (with a few exceptions) show up in a traditional eBay search using the search box on the eBay home page. In order to find store sales items within a store, members must use the search feature on the eBay store home page.

Amazon's WebStores. The setup procedure is quite simple (slightly easier and more user friendly than at eBay stores), and it also includes some bells and whistles that you might not expect. For example, your Web-Store will be hosted on your own website (www.yourstorename.com), a factor that may increase your search engine rankings and increase traffic. You can also easily incorporate Amazon affiliate listings and promotions. Although pricier than the standard eBay store (Amazon Webstores are $59.95 per month), the ease of use, value of being on Amazon and having its security, and feature-rich services makes it worth the extra price. Amazon often offers a free 30-day trial so you can test it out.

RESOURCE
See eBay's homepage (www.ebay.com) or the Amazon Services page (www.amazonservices.com). If you're selling crafts exclusively, check out the stores available at Etsy.com (www.etsy.com).

Making Money From AdSense: Tales of the Gray Googlers

You might not expect that a retired handyman can earn $120,000 from a website, but Jerry Alonzy has managed to pull it off. The income comes from the ads Google places on his Natural Handyman website. "I put in two, maybe three hours a day on the site, and the checks pour in," he says.

In return for placing its ads on websites and blogs, Google pays Web publishers every time one of its ads is clicked. Those clicks help keep Alonzy and his wife living comfortably. "All I need is a laptop and a high-speed Internet connection, and I can live anywhere."

The Internet may be a young person's medium, but the retired and those nearing retirement, such as Alonzy, have found that they can work the Web just as well. Sometimes, such "Gray Googlers" can live a richer, more financially rewarding life than when they were supposedly working.

Take Jerrold Foutz. The former Boeing engineer, 75, started a website a few years ago devoted to one of his passions—switching mode power supplies, which help drive, for instance, the inside of video cameras. He put Google ads on his smpstech.com site four years ago. After just one month, the first Google check was for $800. The second check totaled $2,000. Foutz's experience is not an anomaly.

After Hope Pryor's four kids left home, she learned how to design a Web page. She didn't want it to focus on just her, so she posted some of her favorite recipes on the site. Now, her Cooks Recipes site is bringing in nearly $90,000 yearly, mostly from Google ads.

While the upside of working with AdSense sounds exhilarating, it's not that way for everybody. Al Needham, 74, who runs a site about the care of bees (bees-online.com) from his home near Boston, reaps about $250 a month. "Forget about getting rich overnight," says Alonzy. "It takes time to learn."

 "Gray Googlers strike gold: Some seniors earn surprising income from ads on websites," by Jefferson Graham, October 26, 2007.

Earn Money With Ads and Affiliates

An affiliate program is an arrangement whereby one website pays another for delivering sales or traffic. For example, at one of my websites (www. ndasforfree.com), I have placed affiliate advertising from Amazon for various books (including a few that I have written). If someone clicks an ad and buys one of the books, I will receive 15% of the money received by Amazon. Amazon takes care of the order processing, collecting the money, and shipping the product to the customer. I receive a direct deposit from Amazon for the 15% payment. So, under Amazon's successful affiliate program, you could also earn up to 15% of the revenue if a visitor to your site clicked on an affiliate ad and purchased an Amazon product. Amazon is not the only company with an affiliate program (see the affiliate directories, below). For example, suppose you have a knife-sharpening business. National websites selling cutlery would want to place ads on your site. If one of your visitors clicks on an ad and ends up ordering a fancy blade from a cutlery website, the retailer would pay you a percentage. It's also possible to create affiliate arrangements with local merchants. They can often be managed by creating coupon codes. For example, by entering a code number provided at your website, the buyer gets an additional discount. That also alerts the retailer that the sale was generated by your site.

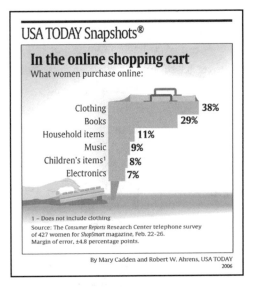

USA TODAY Snapshots®

In the online shopping cart
What women purchase online:

Clothing — 38%
Books — 29%
Household items — 11%
Music — 9%
Children's items[1] — 8%
Electronics — 7%

1 – Does not include clothing
Source: The *Consumer Reports* Research Center telephone survey of 427 women for *ShopSmart* magazine, Feb. 22-26. Margin of error, ±4.8 percentage points.

By Mary Cadden and Robert W. Ahrens, USA TODAY
2006

Earning money from an affiliate program depends on several key points. Ideally, you're looking for something that appeals to visitors of your site, has year-round demand, has a good commission (some pay more than 50%), and is part of a reliable affiliate program. To get started, check one of the affiliate directories, such as Commission

Junction (www.commissionjunction.com), Click Bank (www.clickbank.com), or Associate Programs (www.associateprograms.com).

The major difference between an affiliate program and Google Adsense is that you get paid—usually a few cents—each time someone clicks on one of the Google ads (and is transported to the advertiser's website). In other words, the user does not have to buy anything in order for you to receive your payment. Google AdSense ads appear on the side of your Web pages. Adsense business is booming and Google pays out over $1 billion *per quarter* to its Adsense partners. Still, income is highly speculative and is directly tied to your ability to generate website traffic and click-throughs. Once you sign up to host ads, you'll be given a choice as to which categories, and you can filter ads from competitors, as well.

> **RESOURCE**
> See Darren Rowse's ProBlogger site (www.problogger.com) or read his book, *ProBlogger: Secrets for Blogging Your Way to a Six-Figure Income* (Wiley). For more on affiliates, see Commission Junction (www.commissionjunction.com), Click Bank (www.clickbank.com), or Associate Programs (www.associateprograms.com). Learn more about Google Adsense (www.google.com/adsense). See also *How I Made My First Million on the Internet*, by Ewen Chia (Morgan James) and *Internet Riches: The Simple Money-Making Secrets of Online Millionaires*, by Scott Fox (Amacom).

The (Very) Basics of Driving Traffic to Your Site

As anyone who has started a Web-based business knows, it's not quite as simple as setting up a website or blog and watching the dollars roll in. Success on the Internet requires hypervigilance, patience, a lot of hard work, and luck. The key is driving traffic to your site. So many people make their living by instructing others on how to increase traffic, it's no wonder cynics say the only ones earning money from the Internet gold rush are the people selling pans.

So, how do you get people to come to your website or blog? If your blog is simply a calling card on the Web, then there's no pressure to drive traffic. But if you're trying to generate online sales or would like to profit from AdSense or affiliate marketing, you'll need to attract eyeballs. Here are explanations for some common approaches. If you're serious about pursuing traffic, check out some of the resources, below.

Great Content and Links. The most effective and low-cost method of driving traffic to your site is to create great content that encourages other sites to link to you. For example, Nolo, the publisher of this book, provides extensive free legal information

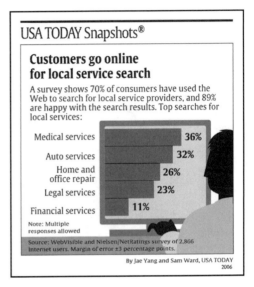

USA TODAY Snapshots®

Customers go online for local service search

A survey shows 70% of consumers have used the Web to search for local service providers, and 89% are happy with the search results. Top searches for local services:

Medical services — 36%
Auto services — 32%
Home and office repair — 26%
Legal services — 23%
Financial services — 11%

Note: Multiple responses allowed

Source: WebVisible and Nielsen/NetRatings survey of 2,866 Internet users. Margin of error ±3 percentage points.

By Jae Yang and Sam Ward, USA TODAY 2006

at its website (www.nolo.com), making it one of the most linked-to legal sites on the Web. By the way, if you're interested in seeing who is linked to your website, type "link:" followed by the address of your website into the Google search engine; for example, type "link:www.nolo.com."

Search Engines and Keywords. Say hello to SEO (search engine optimization), the science of making your website appear high in search engine rankings. Most people find their Web destinations via search engines, which have two types of listings: relevant and sponsored. Relevant listings are the primary search results that appear on the search page. Relevance (the order in which they are listed) is determined by the search engine algorithm, a mathematical formula that uses factors such as the content in a site, its domain name, material in its header (the headline that appears in the bar on top of your browser), information buried in the website code, and the number of sites that are linked to it. (There are numerous ways to increase your relevance as a website and you can pursue those through the resources listed below. Or type "increase traffic website" into a search engine and view the avalanche of results.)

Sponsored links usually appear at the top and in the right margin of the page. You can become a sponsored link by purchasing (or bidding on) keywords at a search company. For example, at Google.com, you can click on the "Advertising Programs" link and buy keywords (Google calls them Adwords) for a setup fee of approximately $5. Keywords are the terms that people type into the search engine. For example, if you had purchased the words "crochet" and "baby," then your ad would pop up when a user searched for crocheted baby hats.

USA TODAY Snapshots®

Women's most-trusted shopping advisers

Friends/family 45%
Online user reviews 13%
News media 11%
Advertising 7%
Manufacturer websites 5%
Retail websites 4%
Salespeople 1%
Other 14%

Source: Consumer Reports National Research Center online survey of 1,264 women, May 22-24, for ShopSmart magazine. Margin of error ± 2.8 percentage points

By Mary Cadden and Dave Merrill, USA TODAY 2006

In reality, keyword buying is a lot more complex. Your choice of keywords is crucial, because if you use terms that are not specific or appropriate, you'll have wasted your money. Often, you must bid for keywords against competitors, and if you have the top bid, you will pay that amount every time someone clicks on your link when it appears in the search engine results.

There's strong sentiment for and against keyword buying. Some marketing people believe that it's useless trying to outbid competitors all the time and that the only one who profits is the search engine company. In addition, keyword prices have escalated in the past few years, making them a more expensive form of marketing.

Other people, particularly in crowded fields, believe that keyword buying is an effective way to rise to the top of the heap. In any case, everyone agrees that if you do buy keywords, you must closely monitor their effectiveness. If you are not getting results from the purchase of certain keywords, ditch those terms—fast. And, of course, if keywords in general are not generating sufficient returns, stop paying for them. For more information, type "Buy keywords" into your search engine.

Finally, some search engines, such as Overture, merge relevance and sponsorship. The more you bid, the more relevant your search results.

Banner Ads. Banner ads are short advertising messages that appear at websites. Like billboards, you can buy this advertising space and place your ads strategically across the Web. Like any form of advertising, you have a challenge: to get the viewer's attention and to motivate the viewer to click though to your site. It's a big challenge for a small ad and we don't recommend them. Your other challenge with a banner ad is to buy space at sites that are likely to be visited by your target audience. You can get some help on the Web at sites such as www.wowbanners.com. Expect to pay a rate of $2 to $3 per every thousand people who see your banner ad. As with keywords, banner ads must be closely monitored for effectiveness. If you're not getting responses, promptly modify or pull the ad.

Affiliate Programs. If you sell one-of-a-kind or niche products at your site, you can offer commissions or rewards to other sites that drive customers to click through and buy those products. For example, a maker of high-end, custom audio equipment may wish to establish an affiliate system with audiophile websites; the maker of safety helmets for young baseball players may wish to affiliate with local Little League sites.

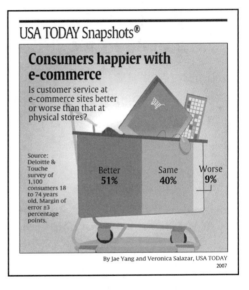

USA TODAY Snapshots®

Consumers happier with e-commerce

Is customer service at e-commerce sites better or worse than that at physical stores?

Source: Deloitte & Touche survey of 1,100 consumers 18 to 74 years old. Margin of error ±3 percentage points.

Better 51% Same 40% Worse 9%

By Jae Yang and Veronica Salazar, USA TODAY 2007

Building a Community. If your customers have something in common, you have an opportunity to unite them in a community at your site. For example, if your business sells soccer supplies, you may want to set aside a portion of your site for a chat room or other community exchange for soccer players in your area, create links for soccer enthusiasts, offer a method of buying discounted tickets to soccer matches, or perhaps even offer an interactive prediction game in which players pick World Cup winners. The key is to take a hint from eBay and unite your customers in a community atmosphere.

RESOURCE
See *Search Engine Optimization: Your Visual Blueprint for Effective Internet Marketing,* by Kristopher B. Jones (Visual); *A Practical Guide to Affiliate Marketing: Quick Reference for Affiliate Managers & Merchants,* by Evgenii Prussakov (AM Navigator); *Ultimate Guide to Google AdWords: How to Access 100 Million People in 10 Minutes,* by Perry Marshall and Bryan Todd (Entrepreneur Press); and *Adwords for Dummies,* by Howie Jacobson (For Dummies).

How to Build a Website in 24 Hours

If free, prefab sites, described above, are not for you, you can build a site from scratch. You'll need three elements:

- **A domain name.** You can buy one at a domain name registrar (assuming your choice is available) or through a hosting company. Expect to pay between $10 and $15 a year.

- **A hosting company.** A hosting company, referred to as an Internet Service Provider or ISP, rents you space on its equipment. You give the host your domain name information (or they'll get the domain name for you) and they broadcast your website for the world to see. Expect to pay $5 to $50 a month for web hosting, depending on the bells and whistles.

- **Website development software.** This is what you use to create your website. If website construction is not your thing, you can hire a website developer or use an ISP such as GoDaddy.com that provides templates.

How to Place Google Ads on Your Website

1. Start with a great topic. Search for it on Google and see if others have a similar idea.

2. You'll need a website. Google has two places to create sites for free: pages.google.com and Blogger.com. Blogger is the easier and faster route. During the creation process, Google will ask if you'd like to add Google ads (AdSense) to your site. You'll need to fill out a form with an address for payment and agree to certain terms.

3. Once you're in the AdSense system, Google offers tips on how to get the most out of your ads. For instance, it teaches about color patterns. Sites with white backgrounds should use ads with a gray background, and publishers should use colors in ads that already exist on the page. Google also offers tools such as a "competitive ad filter," to make sure the cobbler down the street doesn't end up advertising on your shoe repair site.

4. Google gives you a short, one-sentence code to paste in the background of your site, which in turn talks to Google's computers and puts ads automatically onto your site. (With Blogger and Apple's iWeb tools, the coding is done in the background. You just have to click a button to add AdSense to your site.)

5. Now start writing. The folks whose sites reap the most from AdSense have thousands of pages of content. The more pages, the more opportunities for ads and clicks. "If you write for your audience and give them information that's useful and helpful, Google does the rest," says Gail Bjork, who runs the Digicamhelp site.

6. AdSense publisher and author Joel Comm says the next step is to figure out the best place on your page for the ads. "You have to have the ads in a place where they can be seen."

 "So you want to start a site with Google ads," by Jefferson Graham, October 26, 2007.

Building a Store From Scratch. An online store is like a jukebox; it has to look good on the outside but also house some complex inner mechanics. Buyers need to see images of items, fill shopping carts, pay with credit cards, and process orders. If you're building a store from scratch, you'll have to go through the same basic steps as you would for typical sites described above—get a domain name, design your site, and locate an ISP—with one twist: You need to incorporate a shopping cart and credit card payment system. There's a simple solution (see the discussion of PayPal and Google Checkout, above), but if you want buyers to pay you directly through your own credit card merchant account, you've got some programming tasks ahead of you. For more information on shopping cart providers, type "shopping cart services" into a search engine. These companies will handle all of your back-end details and deposit payments into your account.

Dealing With Developers

If you can't, or don't want to, deal with website creation, then get a developer to do it for you. Expect to pay between $500 to $2,000 for a basic site (five to ten website pages). Developers may also assist you on a regular basis by offering Web hosting and regular maintenance. Keep in mind that websites are not static; they need to change as your business changes. So unless you set up a system to update the site yourself, you'll have to keep returning to a developer for every fix. The best solution: Have the developer set up the site and then teach you how to update it. There's an added benefit of using developers: They are often savvy in methods of popularizing sites and you may benefit from their online marketing and traffic-driving knowledge.

RESOURCE

If you're creating a site from scratch and want your own domain name, consider GoDaddy (www.godaddy.com), one of the least expensive ISPs. See also *Creating Web Sites: The Missing Manual*, by Matthew MacDonald (Pogue Press).

Where's the Banana?

Many books have been written about the art and science of creating websites. One of the most popular (and shortest) is Seth Godin's *The Big Red Fez: How to Make Any Website Better* (Free Press). According to Godin, Internet users are like the performing monkey with the red fez: They'll do tricks for you as long as they can see the reward—the banana. On a Web page, unless the banana is obvious —the user recognizes it within three seconds—you've probably lost business. In other words, don't provide too many choices and don't obscure your banana with too many drop-down menus or flashy but slow-to-load graphics. Focus on what's working the best at your site and make it prominent and easy to find; for example, at Amazon, you'll have no trouble recognizing and clicking on the blue box marked "Ready to Buy?"

Basic Legal Rules When Going Online

Many sites post "terms and conditions" somewhere on the site. Do you need them, too? Maybe. If your site sells goods, you may need notices regarding credit card use, refunds, and returns (known as "transaction conditions"). For example, you might want to announce that your business will accept returns up to 30 days after purchase. You may also want to include disclaimers—statements that inform customers that you won't be liable for certain kinds of losses they might incur. For example, you may disclaim responsibility for losses that result if pottery breaks when a customer ships it back for return.

Rules for Refunds

The Federal Trade Commission's Mail or Telephone Order Merchandise Rule, also known as the 30-Day Rule, imposes basic shipping and refund rules on businesses. When you advertise merchandise on eBay and don't say anything about when you plan to ship, you're expected to ship within 30 days from when you receive the payment and all the information needed to fill the order. If your listing does state when you'll ship the merchandise—for example, within two days of payment—you must have a reasonable basis for believing you can meet this shipping deadline.

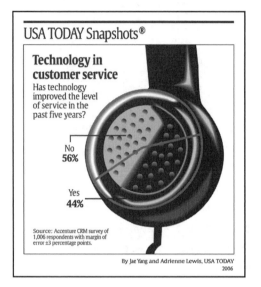

USA TODAY Snapshots®

Technology in customer service
Has technology improved the level of service in the past five years?

No **56%**

Yes **44%**

Source: Accenture CRM survey of 1,006 respondents with margin of error ±3 percentage points.

By Jae Yang and Adrienne Lewis, USA TODAY
2006

If it will take longer than 30 days for you to ship (or longer than you promised), you have a choice:

- You can ask for the customer's consent to the delay. If you can't get consent, you must, without being asked, refund the money the customer paid you for the unshipped merchandise.

- You can simply cancel the order, notify the customer, and refund the payment.

Keep a record of how you notified the customer about the delay, whether by email, phone, fax, or regular mail; when you gave it; and how the customer responded.

Not every business needs an unlimited return policy, but we recommend that you establish a customer-friendly policy of some sort and that you communicate it to your customers.

Before you draft that policy, keep in mind the legal rules. You don't have to give a refund unless:

- You broke the sales contract—for example, your goods were defective.
- You have a policy that allows a refund for returns.

If you want to provide refunds and impose conditions on when merchandise can be returned, post your return and refund policy prominently with your listing or at your online store or website. A typical policy might require the customer to return the merchandise within 30 days for a refund.

State rules on refunds. A few states have laws regarding refunds. It's not always clear whether these laws apply to online retailers doing business with residents of these states. California's law seems to apply to Internet transactions because it applies to "other sellers of goods at retail, and mail order sellers which sell goods at retail in California." New York's law is silent on the issue. So far, there have been no cases enforcing this issue but to err on the conservative side, sellers dealing with residents of these states should consider abiding by the retail rules as follows:

- **California.** You must post your refund policy unless you offer a full cash refund or credit refund within seven days of purchase. If you don't post your policy as required, the customer is entitled to return the goods for a full refund within 30 days of purchase.
- **Florida.** If you don't offer refunds, that fact must be posted. If the statement isn't posted, the customer can return unopened, unused goods within seven days of purchase.
- **New York.** If you offer cash refunds, that policy must be posted, and you must give the refund within 20 days of purchase.
- **Virginia.** If you don't offer a full cash refund or credit within 20 days of purchase, you must post your policy.

Other Terms and Conditions

Here are some other items you may want to include at your website or online store.

Disclaimers. You may want to include disclaimers—statements that inform customers that you won't be liable for certain kinds of losses they might incur. For example, you may disclaim responsibility for losses that result if pottery breaks when a customer ships it back for return.

Privacy. If you're gathering information from your customers, including credit card information, you should post a privacy policy detailing how this information will be used or not used. Yahoo!'s privacy policy is a good example of a broad, easy-to-understand policy. Whatever policy you adopt, be consistent, and if you're going to change it, make an effort to notify your customers by email of the change.

Chats and Postings. If your website provides space for chats or postings from the Web-surfing public, you'll want to limit your liability from offensive or libelous postings or similar chat room comments. There are three things you can do. First, regularly monitor all postings and promptly take down those you think are offensive or libelous. Second, if a third party asks you to remove a posting, remove it while you investigate. If you determine—after speaking with an attorney— that you're entitled to keep the post, then you can put it back up. Third, include a disclaimer on your site that explains you don't endorse and aren't responsible for the accuracy or reliability of statements made by third parties. This won't shield you from claims, but it may minimize your financial damages if you're involved in a lawsuit over the posting.

Copyrights and Trademarks. Include notices regarding copyright and trademark—for example, "Copyright © 2006 RichandAndrea.com" or "DEAR RICH is a trademark of Richard Stim."

Kids. If you're catering to an audience under 13 years old, special rules apply. You should learn more about dealing with children at the Federal Trade Commission website, www.ftc.gov/kidzprivacy.

Managing Your Money

When businessman Monty Burns of *The Simpsons* was given the opportunity to buy eternal happiness for a dollar, he kept the dollar, believing that it would make him "happier." Hmm?

Perhaps that sort of financial decision making works for some businesspeople—after all, Monty is the man who said, "What good is money if it can't inspire terror in your fellow man?"—but for most of us, sound decision making is essential when making financial choices. The bottom line is that no matter how small your side business, you will need to properly manage your money. Don't worry. You don't need a degree in economics. (Even high school dropouts like Richard Branson, Walt Disney, and Coco Chanel learned bookkeeping and accounting chores.)

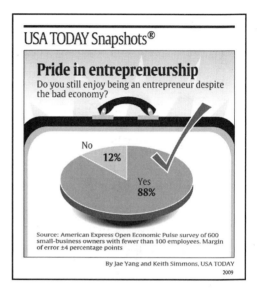

USA TODAY Snapshots®

Pride in entrepreneurship
Do you still enjoy being an entrepreneur despite the bad economy?

No 12%

Yes 88%

Source: American Express Open Economic Pulse survey of 600 small-business owners with fewer than 100 employees. Margin of error ±4 percentage points

By Jae Yang and Keith Simmons, USA TODAY
2009

Here's a hassle-free explanation that won't require too many number-crunching skills.

Record Keeping and Bookkeeping

Bookkeeping—at least in terms of the IRS requirements—doesn't require that you hire an accountant or use bookkeeping software. As long as you can accurately state your income and expenses on your tax forms (and you've got the records necessary to prove that you're correct), you've satisfied the IRS.

You will need to use standardized bookkeeping procedures if you plan on having employees, carrying an inventory, incurring lots of expenses, and (hopefully), enjoying lots of sales.

Whether or not you *need* to use formal bookkeeping, you'll find it a lot easier and more efficient to run your side business with some sort of record-keeping system, preferably on a computer. These records will make your business more profitable by helping you:

- identify every tax deduction you're entitled to take and prepare your tax returns quickly and accurately

- recognize problems early (such as customers who aren't paying on time)

- maintain your cash flow at acceptable levels

- figure out whether it's time to raise (or lower) your prices, and

- if you have more success than expected, to put together the financial reports you need to get loans and investment dollars.

If you're an accounting illiterate and you've been dreading having to finally deal with business bookkeeping, don't worry. Even if you hid in the back of the algebra class, there are simple accounting solutions available to you. Here's how to proceed if the following describes you.

Issue: "I don't want to deal with numbers (except to periodically review financial information)." **Solution:** If your side business is small and easy to manage, you can probably avoid serious number crunching and simply do periodic reviews of your finances. You may even get by with a basic PayPal account and a checkbook. But if your side business is more than that, you should consider hiring someone, like a bookkeeper or an accountant, to handle your numbers. By the way, accounting costs are tax deductible.

Issue: "I want to handle some or all of it." **Solution:** Buy one of the many wonderful software financial or accounting programs and become familiar with it. If you're not sure about how to get started, hire someone to install it—for example your bookkeeper, accountant, or a qualified expert—so that you end up with the proper reports and charts customized for your accounts.

Although we believe you will ultimately have an easier time managing your side business with computer software, there are plenty of noncomputer resources for managing business finances including:

- IRS Publication 583, *Starting a Business and Keeping Records*, free at www.irs.gov. This is a handy guide to basic bookkeeping.
- *The Accounting Game: Basic Accounting Fresh From the Lemonade Stand*, by Darrell Mullis and Judith Orloff (Sourcebooks). This is a fun, simplified explanation of accounting for beginners.
- *Accounting and Finance for Small Business Made Easy*, by Robert Low (Entrepreneur Press). Low demystifies accounting mumbo jumbo.
- *Accounting for Dummies*, by John A. Tracy (Wiley). Tracy creates easy-to-grasp explanations of business financing principles.
- *Minding Her Own Business: The Self-Employed Woman's Guide to Taxes and Recordkeeping*, by Jan Zobel (Sphinx). This book provides detailed examples (and it's not just for women).
- The Business Owner's Toolkit (www.toolkit.cch.com), a site that offers plenty of helpful, free information. Click "Managing Your Business Finances" for a crash course in basic accounting principles.

Accounting and Bookkeeping

What's the difference between accounting and bookkeeping? Accounting is the process of managing and forecasting a business's finances. An accountant advises a business and prepares financial reports. Bookkeeping is utilized in accounting; it refers only to the recording and maintenance of your financial records. A bookkeeper inputs information and keeps your accounts up to date.

Accounting Methods

The IRS doesn't require a specific accounting method, but it does require businesses to use a system that accurately reflects their income and expenses.

The two common ways to account for your income and expenses are the cash method and the accrual method (and some businesses use a hybrid). According to a recent survey, 41% of small business owners use the cash method, 17% used accrual, 13% used a hybrid, and a surprising 28% did not know what system they used (attributed to the fact that these owners did not have a "hands-on approach" to record keeping).

The cash method. Using the cash method, you record income when you actually receive it and expenses when you actually pay them. For example, if you complete a project in December 2009 but don't get paid until March 2010, you record the income in March 2010. Similarly, if you buy a digital camera for your business on credit, you record the expense not when you charge the camera and take it home, but when you pay the bill. (The IRS won't let you manipulate your income by, for example, not cashing a client's check until the next year; you must report income when it becomes available to you, not when you actually decide to deal with it.)

The accrual method. Under the accrual method, you record income as you earn it and expenses as you incur them. For example, if you complete a project in December 2009, that's when you record the income you expect to receive from the project, no matter when the client actually gets around to paying you. (If the client never puts the check in the mail, you can eventually deduct the money as a bad debt.) And if you charge some furniture, you record the expense on the day of purchase, not when you pay the bill.

Which method is better? We recommend the cash method for your side business. It is much easier to use; most of us deal with our personal finances this way, so it's a system we're familiar with. It also gives you a clear picture of your actual cash on hand at any point in time. The accrual method can't tell you how much cash you've got, but it provides a more accurate picture of your business's overall financial health, particularly if your clients or customers are pretty good about paying their bills. It will show money that you've obligated yourself to pay, so you'll know that you can't count on using that money for other purposes. It will also show money you can look forward to receiving (again, if your customers pay you as promised). For more information, check out IRS Publications 334, *Tax Guide for Small Business*, and 538, *Accounting Periods and Methods*, both available at www.irs.gov.

What Is Cash Flow and Why Is It Essential?

You've probably heard people complain about cash flow and maybe wondered what exactly that means. Simply put, the money that comes in and goes out of your side business is your cash flow. Business cash flow is really no different from personal cash flow. For example, when you're in a furniture store trying to decide whether to spend a portion of your paycheck on a new sofa, that's a cash flow decision. If you use the money on the sofa, you may not have enough to pay for your new hubcaps (or that beloved daily cappuccino at Starbucks).

USA TODAY Snapshots®

Key factors in buying tech items

More than one-quarter of respondents say they have become more accepting of new technology. Top factors considered when acquiring new technology:

Ease of use	61%
Customer service	58%
No-hassle installation	57%
Getting a thorough understanding of how it works	53%
Warranty	50%

Note: Multiple responses allowed
Source: Harris Interactive online survey of 1,174 adults age 18 and over. Margin of error ±3 percentage points.

By Jae Yang and Alejandro Gonzalez, USA TODAY 2006

Proper cash flow management is the key to profitability for your side business (and for its survivability). Think of cash flow as your business's lifeblood. If it is interrupted—and this is true even for highly profitable ventures—it can lead to a business's cardiac arrest.

Four Common Causes of Cash Flow Problems

Four common reasons that businesses have cash flow problems are:

Accounts receivable are late. When people are not paying you in a timely manner, you'll always be short of cash. Are you reluctant to approach your customers? We discuss how to deal with collections later in this chapter.

Inventory is turning slowly. Inventory—the stuff you sell—is cash transformed into products. So, when you're holding unsold inventory, you're really preventing access to cash. In addition, inventory costs create a financial burden. That's why it's sometimes wise to sell inventory at break-even prices rather than have it take up space without generating revenue.

Expenses are not controlled. It may be axiomatic, but your failure to control costs can be a major factor in cash flow problems. Always look for ways to lower expenses. Throughout this book we provide tips on lowering fixed and variable expenses. You'll be surprised: Even the leanest business can shed a few pounds.

Bills are paid before they're due. When possible, we recommend paying your bills early. Often, however, there are benefits to waiting—say, 30 days—and then paying the bill. In fact, in terms of holding on to your cash, it's even better to get longer terms for paying back your suppliers.

Three Side Businesses That Are Prone to Cash Flow Problems

Certain side businesses, by their nature, may have more cash flow challenges than others. Some examples include:

A side business that relies on one customer for all its income. Whether by choice or because of circumstance, sometimes you end up placing all your eggs in one customer's basket. If you find yourself growing quickly with one customer, you may be tempted to terminate smaller accounts. Keep in mind that loyal smaller accounts give a business a constant, reliable source of income even if it is dwarfed by large orders from one customer.

A seasonal business. When it comes to seasonal income, it's not so much a matter of getting paid on time—you already know with some certainty when you'll be paid. The issue is usually whether the lack of income throughout the rest of the year is a problem. If so, you'll need to come up with creative solutions for the other parts of the year.

A side business that relies on sales of one product. Sometimes all you need is one product to hit it big (Snuggies, anyone?) But for many businesses, the one-trick pony approach eventually gets risky. The key with product or service diversification is to be sure the new offerings are central and complementary to the existing business.

Three Keys to Managing Cash Flow

The three tasks (or strategies) for managing cash flow are:

Be prepared. You can never completely avoid cash flow problems—unpredictable and catastrophic events can overtake any side business. The best preparation is to think ahead and if possible, maintain your access to credit.

Know your funding options. We'd like you to avoid borrowing money for your side business, but if you borrow money, ask yourself whether you are doing so because of a temporary negative cash flow or because of a fundamental problem with your side business. If you don't know the difference, you could find yourself shoveling your way out of a mountain of debt. We provide more information later in this chapter.

Always know your numbers. A reliable bookkeeping system can prevent (and predict) many financial problems.

Five Accounting Principles You Need to Know

You're probably already operating with a simple easy-to-manage bookkeeping system. So, our guess is that you won't need to know many accounting principles to manage a small side business. But if you plan on growing it, it will help to understand these five basic principles.

Assets and Liabilities

Assets are your "pluses," the things your side business owns and is owed—for example, cash, inventory, accounts due, and other property. Liabilities are your "minuses," the business obligations or things that are owed—for example, tax payments, repayments to investors, or money owed to banks. Assets and liabilities figure into the business's balance sheet—a snapshot of your business at a given time. A balance sheet adds up the assets and liabilities in two separate columns. As the name implies, the columns must balance—that is, they should equal each other.

Equity and Debt

Equity is the money or property invested and retained in the business by the owners (sometimes referred to as owner's equity). Debt—the loans, lines of credit, and any other borrowing you've done—refers to money that must be repaid, usually with interest, over a fixed period of time.

Accounts Receivable and Accounts Payable

Accounts receivable are the amounts you are owed from sales of your products or services. Some retail businesses, because they receive payment immediately, have little or no accounts receivable. Accounts payable are amounts you owe to vendors and suppliers, as well as any other short-term bills—for example, payments for inventory, supplies, or other goods or services. Loans and similar interest-bearing debts are not included in accounts payable. Monitoring receivables and payables is a key element in cash flow management.

Income Statements

In order to avoid the mistake of looking at a payment and guessing at the profit, business owners use an income statement—a statement that provides a line-by-line breakdown of revenue and the various sums that are subtracted from the revenue to determine profit. Most popular accounting software programs can generate income statements.

Cash Flow Statements

A cash flow statement summarizes all the cash coming in and going out of a business during a specific period by analyzing cash in three classes: operations (sales and operating expenses), financing activities (loans and equity), and investing activities (ownership of real estate, securities, and nonoperating assets). The challenge with cash flow statements is they sometimes become too cumbersome to decipher.

What Is Forecasting?

Depending on how crunchy you want your numbers, you may want to consider forecasting. Financial forecasting helps you predict the cost of your products or services, the amount of sales revenue, and your anticipated profit. If your business is not already off the ground, financial forecasting can help you predict how much you'll have to invest or borrow.

Obviously, financial forecasting depends on your type of business— that is, whether you are a retail business, service business, manufacturing or wholesale business, or a project development business (such as real estate rehabilitation, or "flipping," in which you overhaul one house at a time).

Forecasting is always easier if you've been in business for a little while, because you have months (or years) of actual revenue and expenses upon which to base your forecasts. If you don't have any history, this section can help you get started.

First, forecasting is not essential for many microbusinesses. Alternatively, you may already have your own method of forecasting profits and expenses.

Second, don't be intimidated. Financial forecasting is not so hard to digest. It's a matter of making educated guesses as to how much money you will take in and how much you will spend, then using these estimates to calculate how and when your business will be profitable. The numbers you use are not written in stone. You can alter them to create "what if" scenarios.

Again, many side-business owners won't need or want to do forecasting because they'll have their pulse on the revenue and expenses. But if you're looking to grow, you may want a basic understanding of financial projections, as described here.

The Break-Even Analysis

This analysis tells you how much revenue you'll need each week or month to break even. To calculate it, you'll need to do a little paperwork, starting with two estimates for:

- **Fixed costs,** also known as overhead, which usually include rent, insurance, and other regular, set expenses.
- **Gross profit,** which is what's left after you deduct the direct costs for each sale.

For example, let's say you're reselling imported scarves on eBay. If you paid $15 for each scarf and resold each for $25, your gross profit is $10 per scarf. In order to determine your gross profit percentage, you divide your profit by the selling price. The result, in this case, is 40%: $10 (profit) ÷ $25 (selling price) = 40%.

To calculate your break-even amount, divide your monthly overhead expenses by your profit percentage (as a decimal). For example, if your eBay shop has fixed monthly costs of $200 and your profit percentage is 40%, then you need sales revenue of $500 a month to break even: $200 (fixed monthly costs) ÷ 0.40 (profit percentage as a decimal) = $500.

So, as a practical matter, if you were selling scarves at $25 a piece, you would need to sell 20 scarves a month to break even: 20 scarves x $25 a scarf = $500.

If this amount is below your anticipated sales revenue, then you're facing a loss—and you'll need to lower expenses or increase sales to break even.

The Profit and Loss Forecast

In your profit and loss forecast, you refine the sales and expense estimates that you used for your break-even analysis into a formal, month-by-month projection of your business's profit for one or two years of operation. It's basically a spreadsheet that details your expected expenses and revenue on a month-by-month basis. Most popular accounting software programs can prepare these forecasts.

Cash Flow Projection

Earlier, we described a cash flow statement—a look at the movement of cash during a specific period. The cash flow projection attempts to predict your cash flow needs. Cash flow projections are useful for every business, but they're particularly helpful if you have not yet begun operating. To make your cash flow projection, you'll have to prepare a spending plan, setting out items your business needs to buy and expenses you will need to pay.

Should You Separate Business and Personal?

A lot of people pay their side-business expenses with a personal check or credit card and deposit side-business income into their household checking account, along with a spouse's salary, tax refunds, client reimbursements, inheritances, lottery winnings, and so on. As long as you keep careful records, this will work just fine.

But if you're growing your side business, you should consider keeping separate accounts for your business and personal expenses and income. Even if you have to pay a bit extra to open more accounts, it will simplify your bookkeeping greatly and, if you operate a business under a name other than your real name, it will make depositing checks easier. You could also use a no-fee business credit card or,

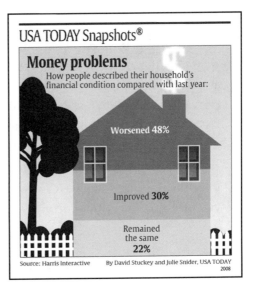

USA TODAY Snapshots®

Money problems
How people described their household's financial condition compared with last year:

Worsened 48%

Improved 30%

Remained the same 22%

Source: Harris Interactive   By David Stuckey and Julie Snider, USA TODAY 2008

if you can't find that, simply use one of your personal credit cards solely for business. That way, you'll have no trouble calculating your interest deduction.

Raising Money for Your Business

The good news about most side businesses is that they don't require a great deal of capital. For that reason, we hope you have not exhausted your savings to start or run your side business.

It is possible that you may need more money to expand (or maybe just to keep the business running). You probably won't get that money from your local bank or from outside investors (strangers)—fewer than one in five small businesses are able to fund themselves from these sources. Instead, you should expect that any money you need will come from credit cards or family and friends.

What's the Difference? Equity vs. Debt

There are two ways to get money for your side business: Borrow it (debt financing) or find somebody to invest in it (equity financing). Here's how it works: Let's say a wealthy aunt loves your side business and wants to help (you sell reconditioned hearing aids via your website). Your aunt can lend you the money under the terms of a loan agreement (sometimes referred to as a note), or she can purchase a partial ownership of your business from you. In order to accomplish the latter, you must have a business entity that can accommodate that kind investment—generally, a limited liability company or corporation.

The disadvantage of a loan is that you owe money; the disadvantage of investment is that you give up a portion of your ownership interest and you may also lose some control over how your business is run.

Borrowing With Credit Cards

In the heyday of easy credit—back in 2007—the average U.S. consumer had access to $12,190 from credit cards. So it's easy to see why half of the nation's start-ups were funded with plastic. Of course, even after the 2008 economic downturn, credit cards are still with us and banks are not afraid to disburse them freely to credit-worthy individuals.

We don't need to dwell on the downsides—you're probably already aware that credit card companies charge high interest rates and extraordinary penalties. And if you miss a payment on one card, all of your cards can raise their interest rates. You can easily get in over your head. When you take a cash advance, you'll encounter more unbearable fees and usually no grace period, which means you pay interest from the day you take the advance, even if you pay off your balance within a month.

In general, we advise against using credit cards to fund your side business. Of course, our advice ignores the reality of operating a small business. Mini-entrepreneurs depend on plastic. So, is there any way to alleviate the negatives? Here are a few suggestions.

When shopping for a card, be wary of teaser rates (low introductory rates that jump after a few months) and check the grace period (the number of days you're charged interest on purchases). Many companies have been shortening their grace period for purchases from 30 to 20 days. Shop around for perks, like airline miles, travel discounts, or other purchasing credits. Always compare the periodic rates that will be used to calculate the finance charge. You can find rates at websites comparing current credit offers (type "credit card compare" into a search engine).

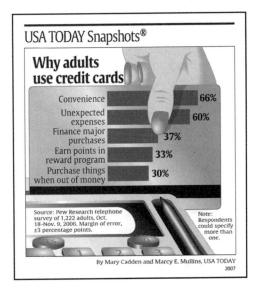

USA TODAY Snapshots®

Why adults use credit cards

Convenience	66%
Unexpected expenses	60%
Finance major purchases	37%
Earn points in reward program	33%
Purchase things when out of money	30%

Source: Pew Research telephone survey of 1,222 adults, Oct. 18-Nov. 9, 2006. Margin of error, ±3 percentage points.

Note: Respondents could specify more than one.

By Mary Cadden and Marcy E. Mullins, USA TODAY 2007

Don't charge business expenses if your credit card balances are greater than 80% of your credit limits; you've already got a credit card problem. One other thought: Bankruptcy laws make it much harder to get rid of credit card debts, even if you file for bankruptcy, particularly if your income is greater than the median income for your state.

Bank Loans

The old saying about bank loans—that you can qualify for a bank loan only when you don't need it—unfortunately rings true. The more speculative your side business (the more it requires imagination to envision its success), the less likely you will get a loan unless you have assets beyond the amount of the loan. Which leads us to the bigger question: What motivates a bank to loan money?

The decision is traditionally based on the five "Cs" of credit—capacity (how you intend to repay), collateral (what assets do you have to guarantee payment?), character (are you trustworthy?), capital (how much have you invested in your business?), and conditions (what's the business climate?). Practically speaking, you're much more likely to qualify if you can personally guarantee the loan or you can secure the loan with property equal to the value of the loan. You're less likely to qualify if your cash flow is erratic or the forecast for your industry is poor.

Why do banks reject loan applications? Sometimes it's because the person starting the business doesn't offer enough collateral or refuses to make a personal guarantee. Collateral refers to the assets that you pledge for the repayment of a loan. A personal guarantee means that the borrower guarantees repayment from personal assets, in addition to business assets. Another common reason for rejection is that the business owner has a checkered credit history.

SBA Loans

If you're interested in a bank loan but you're not sure if you qualify or how to proceed, you may want to check out the Small Business Administration (SBA). The SBA does not make loans; it guarantees up to 85% of the amount you borrow from someone else in the event of default. Beware, though: Despite SBA support, lenders sometimes require collateral or personal guarantees from the business owner for all (or a portion) of the loan. In other words, getting an SBA-guaranteed loan is often as difficult as getting a regular bank loan. To find out more, check out the SBA website (www.sba.gov). The most helpful resource for preparing an SBA loan application is *SBA Loans: A Step-by-Step Guide*, by Patrick O'Hara (Wiley).

State Lending Assistance

Your side business may qualify for other lending sources, including:

- **Business Development Centers (BDCs).** Approximately 20 states offer SBA-style loan assistance to their residents. Check your state government website to find out whether your state offers BDC help.
- **Local development funds.** Many communities offer small loans or grants to businesses in order to encourage development. Check with your city or county government.
- **State loans.** Some states lend money directly to small businesses to encourage certain industries within the state. For example, Hawaii intends to encourage technology companies by offering loans through the Hawaii Strategic Development Corporation (HSDC). Check your state's website for more information.

Borrowing From Family and Friends

Family and friends are usually more comfortable lending money than buying an interest in your company. A loan is a straightforward matter. But ownership (often in the form of shares in your corporation) often seems abstract and risky. If you're going to borrow from family and friends (or from any individual, for that matter), make sure you do it with the appropriate formalities: Sign a promissory note, calculate interest and principal, and set up a payment schedule. If you don't, you may find yourself embroiled in money disputes over Thanksgiving dinner.

You can easily draft your own promissory note (forms are available from Nolo, the publisher of this book, as well as from other providers on the Internet). You can calculate interest and payments using amortization calculators that are easily found online.

You can also get help making a loan more businesslike from Virgin Money (www.virginmoneyus.com). Virgin Money doesn't lend money —it facilitates loans. A Virgin Money loan specialist examines your loan, helps to prepare a legally binding agreement (with secured collateral, if required), and then creates a repayment schedule. The company also manages the payment process through automatic electronic debits and credits and will send payment reminders to the borrower. Virgin Money must be doing something right: The company has managed over $200 million in loans.

Social Lending Networks

What if obtaining a business loan were as simple as posting an item on eBay? That's the goal of social lending network sites such as Prosper (www.prosper.com) and Lending Club (www.lendingclub.com). Unlike sites like Virgin Money, which facilitate loans between family and friends, social lending networks allow the business seeking money to post its needs at the site (usually up to $25,000) and then—assuming the borrower meets certain credit standards—lenders can make offers at various interest rates. We have not used either site so we cannot endorse either but both have been around for a few years and Lending Club reportedly has become so popular that at various times, it has stopped accepting new lenders. If you run a search listing both sites, you can also read comparisons of their interest rates and practices. A third site, Zopa (www.zopa.com), launched internationally in 2005 and more recently began offering services in the United States.

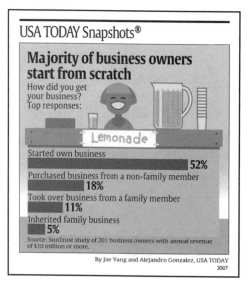

USA TODAY Snapshots®

Majority of business owners start from scratch

How did you get your business? Top responses:

Started own business 52%
Purchased business from a non-family member 18%
Took over business from a family member 11%
Inherited family business 5%

Source: SunTrust study of 201 business owners with annual revenue of $10 million or more.

By Jae Yang and Alejandro Gonzalez, USA TODAY 2007

What Is Angel Investing?

Angel investing is a hot topic on the Internet and is sometimes portrayed as a magic bullet for businesses that need money. Don't be fooled. There's nothing particularly angelic about the relationship. Basically, it involves finding and convincing a wealthy individual—someone willing to take a risk—to buy a chunk of your business (but not enough to take it away from you). An angel investor usually invests close to home, insists on direct involvement in the business, and wants a high rate of return (20% to 50%). Angels are also looking for a great team in much the same way that a gambler looks at the horse, the jockey, the trainer, and the owner.

Since most side businesses are too small to attract the attention of an angel investor, you aren't likely to bother with angels. But if you're curious to learn more, review the material at Active Capital (formerly ACE-NET) (www.activecapital.org), one of the oldest and most well-established sites for entrepreneurs seeking private investment. Companies such as FundingUniverse (www.fundinguniverse.com), PlanHeaven (www.planheaven.com), FundingPost (www.fundingpost.com), and Go4Funding (www.go4funding.com) offer variations on the angel brokering theme.

Getting Paid

The most common reason for cash flow problems is that a customer fails to pay you on time (or at all). When that happens, you have to spend time chasing the deadbeat and you may have to delay paying suppliers, contractors, and yourself. You didn't create a side business to hassle someone over payments. What's a business owner to do?

Unfortunately, getting paid is part of doing business, and you'll have to master the details. Fortunately, with a little preparation you can prevent some late payments, bounced checks, and credit card fraud;

and you can also develop the business radar that lets you know when an account is headed for collection. Below, we'll discuss the ways businesses get paid and what to do if you don't.

Invoiced Accounts

If you're a professional service provider—for example, a lawyer or an accountant—or you sell products to a wholesaler (a company that places your goods in retail accounts), then you must invoice your customers. An invoice is a bill that sets the terms for payment. Most invoices require payment within 30, 60, or 90 days.

When you invoice a customer, your business is extending credit. You may not feel like you're extending credit—after all, you're just waiting for payment—but from a legal perspective, you're making an unsecured loan. (A secured loan is one which the borrower would pledge property as a collateral for the loan.) The problem with unsecured loans is that they're just that—unsecured. If the business doesn't have the money, it won't do any good to sue, because there will be nothing to recover. If the business goes bankrupt, you're out of luck.

Most of the time, there's no problem extending credit. If you do have doubts about a new business customer, you can check on creditworthiness by having them complete a credit reference form (and checking the results). A good credit reference form should require information about who is in charge of the business, who to contact when problems develop, how much credit the applicant is seeking, other firms with which the company has done business on credit, and any other financial information required for making your decision. If it's a big account and you're investing a lot of resources in it, it may be worth it to pay for credit research from a company such as Dun & Bradstreet (www.dnb.com), BusinessCreditUSA (www.businesscreditusa.com), or Equifax (www.equifax.com).

When you get the information, how do you tell whether the customer is a credit risk? Collections expert Timothy Paulsen suggests separating patterns from single events. If a customer has one or two minor credit blemishes—perhaps the result of an unexpected growth spurt—that should not necessarily be the basis of denying credit. That is different from evidence that indicates the client or customer just doesn't like to pay bills.

The greatest risk in extending credit is to throw all of your business to one big account. The obvious problem with that strategy is that you're at risk of losing a lot of money if the big account has financial problems or goes bankrupt. For that reason, avoid ditching smaller accounts because of large orders from one customer. Loyal smaller accounts give a business a constant, reliable source of income.

When you write your invoice, provide an accurate, clear statement of the transaction and request that the customer contact you if there are problems. That request may make it harder for a slow-paying account to later excuse its delinquent behavior.

Got Cash?

Besides a bank wire transfer, cash is probably the most reliable way to get paid. Worried about counterfeit bills? No need. According to the Department of the Treasury, only nine out of every million bills are counterfeit.

Checks

You're probably aware of the typical precautions you can take to avoid bounced checks, but because 450 million rubber checks appear each year, we'll remind you anyway. Don't take checks without seeing a photo ID. Reject the check if it lacks the person's name, is postdated, or it's a two-party check (a check written by someone other than your prospective buyer).

Also, don't accept a check for less than the full amount owed that says "Payment in Full." In some states, if you deposit the check, especially if the amount owed is in dispute, you may have wiped out the balance owed.

Getting Paid With Credit Cards

If you're operating a bricks-and-mortar business (not online) and want to accept credit cards, you'll need to establish a merchant account, set up through a bank associated with a credit card processing company, which will handle the actual credit card orders. You must pay application fees, which can range from $200 to $600.

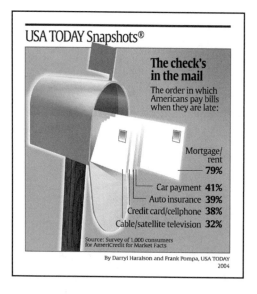

USA TODAY Snapshots®

The check's in the mail

The order in which Americans pay bills when they are late:

Mortgage/rent — **79%**
Car payment **41%**
Auto insurance **39%**
Credit card/cellphone **38%**
Cable/satellite television **32%**

Source: Survey of 1,000 consumers for AmeriCredit for Market Facts

By Darryl Haralson and Frank Pompa, USA TODAY 2004

The percentage you have to pay Visa or MasterCard (usually 2% to 3% of sales) depends on your expected sales revenue and the policies of the bank. Although the percentage takes a cut from your revenue, there's an upside to it—getting paid by credit card means you can skip credit checks and not be bothered by collections. Because banks may reject your merchant application if it seems unrealistic (you're estimating way-high sales revenue), it's wise to estimate conservatively. Expect bank approval to take one to two months.

Getting Paid via PayPal

Many retailers and service providers use PayPal (www.paypal.com) an automated online payment system that enables anyone with an email address to make payments from across the country or around the world. Because the system works so well, it is the clearly preferred way to pay for many online purchases. Sending money via PayPal is free, but receiving money may be subject to a fee depending on the type of PayPal account you have.

Although owned by eBay, PayPal can be used in transactions besides those on eBay. You can also use your account to accept payments via your website, regardless of whether you have an eBay account. As part of its Merchant Services program, PayPal offers a free PayPal Shopping Cart system.

Going Online With Credit Cards

If you're taking credit card orders online, you'll need an e-commerce provider who manages your shopping cart and credit card acceptance. The credit card processing is handled by the provider's credit card transaction clearinghouse, a company that collects money from a customer and then pays the credit card companies their percentage of the sales. The balance is then deposited into your bank account within three days.

Credit Card Fraud

In the offline world, where a paying customer must show you the physical credit card, it's sometimes easier to avoid fraud. You have an opportunity to judge the customer's demeanor and (in most states) to verify, by asking for identification, that the customer and card owner are one and the same. If in doubt, you can call the issuing bank and check that the credit card is in good standing.

Although fraud is harder to prevent online, the good news is that credit card transaction clearinghouses use fraud prevention systems that can flag risky transactions—for example, they may use Card Identification Codes, the three- or four-digit numbers that are printed on the back of a credit card in addition to the 16-digit embossed number. Ask your e-commerce provider or credit card transaction clearinghouse about its antifraud protection.

Ten Tips for Collecting Accounts Receivable

In a sense, getting paid is actually an element of your marketing. If you can work with financially troubled clients as they make their way through a rough patch, you may end up with devoted customers for life.

Late-paying customers usually fall into three categories:

- customers who want to pay but, because of real financial problems, can't do it on time

- customers who prefer to delay or juggle payments, and

- customers who will do whatever possible to avoid payment.

For the first two categories, there is hope. You may be able to manage these debts and to convince the debtors to make partial or full payment. This is especially true if you have encouraged customer loyalty and your customers sincerely want to support you. As for the last category, you need to recognize this type as quickly as possible and take serious action—perhaps turning the account over to a collections agency.

Here are ten suggestions for managing your collections.

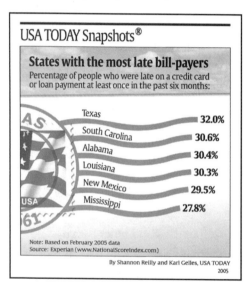

USA TODAY Snapshots®

States with the most late bill-payers
Percentage of people who were late on a credit card or loan payment at least once in the past six months:

Texas — 32.0%
South Carolina — 30.6%
Alabama — 30.4%
Louisiana — 30.3%
New Mexico — 29.5%
Mississippi — 27.8%

Note: Based on February 2005 data
Source: Experian (www.NationalScoreIndex.com)

By Shannon Reilly and Karl Gelles, USA TODAY 2005

Collection Tip #1: Get Busy and Stay at It

According to a survey by the Commercial Collection Agency Association (www.ccascollect.com), after only three months, the probability of collecting a delinquent account drops to 73%. After six months, it's down to 57%. After one year, the chance of ever collecting on a past due account is a dismal 29%. Send bills promptly and rebill monthly. There's no need to wait for the end of the month. Send past due notices promptly once an account is overdue.

Collection Tip #2: Read About Collections

Debt collectors can offer helpful tips and you can learn many of them by reading either *Collections Made Easy*, by Carol Frischer (Career Press), or *Paid in Full*, by Timothy R. Paulsen (Advantage), both of which are friendly, succinct, and helpful.

Collection Tip #3: Don't Harass Debtors

It's rarely a successful strategy and it's sometimes illegal. If a customer asks that you stop calling, then stop calling. If a customer asks you to call at another time, find out the right time to call, and call then. Don't leave more than one phone message a day for a debtor, and never leave messages that threaten the debtor or contain statements that put the debtor in a bad light.

Collection Tip #4: Be Direct and Listen

Keep your calls short and be specific. Listen to what the debtor says and keep a log of all of your collections phone calls.

Collection Tip #5: Look for Creative Solutions

If the customer has genuine financial problems, ask what amount they can realistically afford. Consider extending the time for payment if the customer agrees in writing to a new payment schedule. Consider entering into a simple promissory note with the debtor that details the new payment schedule. Call the day before the next scheduled payment is due to be sure the customer plans to respect the agreement.

USA TODAY Snapshots®

Work-life balance tops pay
What is the primary reason you accepted your current position? Top responses:

Work-life balance and flexibility 29%
Compensation 23%
Work culture 13%
Training opportunities 5%
Advancement opportunities 5%

Source: Hudson survey of 1,634 workers who have been in their current positions for at least five years. Margin of error ±3 percentage points.

By Jae Yang and Keith Simmons, USA TODAY 2008

Collection Tip #6: Write Demand Letters

Along with phone calls, send a series of letters that escalate in intensity. You can find sample collection letters (sometimes referred to as "demand letters") online. Save copies of all correspondence with the customer and keep notes of all telephone conversations (in case you hand the matter over to collections or take the customer to court). You can also pay a collection agency a fixed fee to write a series of letters on your behalf. (This is different than turning over the debt to an agency.) For example, Dun & Bradstreet Small Business Solutions (http://smallbusiness.dnb.com) will write a series of three letters for $25.

Collection Tip #7: Deal With Excuses

How can you tell if the customer is simply delinquent with a payment or whether the delinquency is a precursor to bigger financial problems? That is, how can you sift through the excuses given by a debtor without a lie detector? Carol Frischer considers excuses like a puzzle. You must solve each one and then stay a few steps ahead of the next one. If you're given an excuse—the person writing checks is sick this week—then you must determine whether it is true or not. If it turns out not to be true— that is, another excuse arrives the following week—then you should become less tolerant and more aggressive. Always maintain your sense of urgency. For example, if the company is "expecting a big check next week," insist on a partial payment this week and the remainder when the big check arrives.

Collection Tip #8: Offer a One-Time Deep Discount

If an account is fairly large and remains unpaid for an extended period (say six months) and you're doubtful about ever collecting, consider offering in writing a time-limited, deep discount to resolve the matter. This way, the customer has the incentive to borrow money to take advantage of your one-time, never-again offer to settle. You can finalize this with a mutual release and settlement, a legal document that terminates the debt. You can find such forms at Nolo's website (www. nolo.com).

Collection Tip #9: Turn the Account Over to a Collection Agency

Turning a debt over to collections is your last resort. A collection agency will usually pay you 50% (or less) of what it recovers. Of course, in some cases, half is better than nothing. You're likely to want the help of a collection agency when the customer lies to you about the transaction or becomes a serial promise breaker, falsely assuring you on various occasions that payment is on the way. Dun & Bradstreet Small Business Solutions (http://smallbusiness. dnb.com) and other companies offer debt collection services. The Commercial Collection Agency Association (www.ccascollect. com) provides more information on collection agencies.

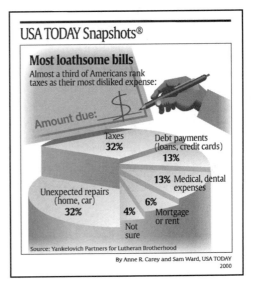

USA TODAY Snapshots®

Most loathsome bills

Almost a third of Americans rank taxes as their most disliked expense:

Amount due:

Taxes **32%**

Debt payments (loans, credit cards) **13%**

13% Medical, dental expenses

Unexpected repairs (home, car) **32%**

6%

4% Mortgage or rent

Not sure

Source: Yankelovich Partners for Lutheran Brotherhood

By Anne R. Carey and Sam Ward, USA TODAY 2000

Collection Tip #10: Consider a Lawsuit

You can also take the debtor to court. Small claims court is inexpensive, though it can take a good chunk of your time. Furthermore, any judgment that you receive may be worthless if the debtor lacks a job or bank account. For an excellent guide to using small claims court and collecting after you win, see *Everybody's Guide to Small Claims Court*, by Ralph Warner (Nolo). You can hire a lawyer for larger debts (say, over $5,000). But beware of filing a lawsuit to chase a debt; your legal fees may exceed the amount owed.

If a Customer Goes Bankrupt

The worse your customer's financial condition, the harder it is to recover any money. When a customer declares bankruptcy, you've got a big problem. A bankruptcy will effectively wipe out your debt unless you're a secured creditor (the customer promised some property to secure your debt). Pursuing a creditor into bankruptcy is often not worth the effort.

International Sales

If you're selling outside the United States, there's only one tip you need: Get paid up front. You don't have the ability to chase down rubles, drachmas, or pesos in a faraway land. These payments can be made by credit card, bank transfers, or bank letters of credit. To avoid confusion about currency conversion, keep your dealings in U.S. dollars. For more information on exporting goods, check out the U.S. Trade Information Center (www.trade. gov/td/tic). ●

USA TODAY Snapshots®

The road rules for cargo

Value of freight from the USA to Canada and Mexico in 2005 (in billions):

Road — $491
Rail — $116
Water — $58
Pipeline — $52
Air — $33

Source: Department of Transportation

By Karl Gelles, USA TODAY
2006

Protecting Personal Assets

D o you have a nagging concern that your personal savings, car, or house will be at risk if your side business incurs a debt or causes an injury? That's possible if:

- **You personally guarantee a loan or other debt, or you use personal assets as collateral for a business loan.** Most lenders condition small business loans upon the business owner's personal guarantee.

- **Your side business causes an injury or loss.** If you have clients who come to your home, you use your automobile for your side business, or your business has inherent risks—you teach paragliding, juggling, or you install solar panels—then your chances of causing personal or property injuries increase and you should be concerned about personal liability. On the other hand, you probably have little risk if you run an eBay business selling used DVDs (unless of course, you're selling pirated DVDs).

You can take any or all of the three tried-and-true approaches to protecting personal assets: You can form a business entity that limits liability, purchase insurance, and/or simply be careful and avoid risks.

Using Business Entities to Limit Liability

Unless you change the status of your sole proprietorship business, it will remain a sole proprietorship—that is, it will be run by you and you will be personally liable for business debts and obligations. That's fine, especially, if your business simply isn't going to run up many debts or run many risks. In that case, you probably don't need to convert from a sole proprietorship to an LLC or a corporation. (Eighteen million small businesses in the United States have not chosen to incorporate or form an LLC.)

LLCs and corporations can shield your personal assets—your house and savings—from many business debts and court judgments, but they may not be necessary for businesses that are low on the liability scale. Insurance may be a better method of protecting assets.

Consider the cost. Forming an LLC or a corporation costs between $500 and $2,000, depending on who does it and in which state it's being formed. Many states impose annual fees, sometimes over $1,000 a year, for maintaining an LLC or a corporation. (California LLCs pay a minimum of $800 a year.)

Bottom line: If you're not that concerned about personal liability, or you believe that insurance can cover any liability, or you're just not that interested in paying the fees or dealing with the additional formalities, an LLC or a corporation is probably not the right choice for your side business.

Still not sure? Below, we provide a basic summary of sole proprietorships, partnerships, LLCs, and corporations.

What Are You? Sole Proprietorship or Partnership?

We'll assume that you're either a sole proprietorship (operating as one-person business) or a general partnership (an informal group of owners). Below we've charted the basics of these types of businesses. As you'll see, what differentiates these business forms are taxation, liability, and formalities (the requirements and costs for forming and maintaining the entity).

Sole Proprietorship

If you're operating by yourself (or maybe with your spouse, see "Can a Husband and Wife Be a Sole Proprietorship?") and you haven't incorporated or formed an LLC, you're a sole proprietorship. A sole proprietorship is the least expensive and easiest way to operate a business.

Sole Proprietorships at a Glance	
Taxation	A sole proprietorship is a pass-through entity. Your profits (and losses) pass through the business entity, and you pay taxes on any profits on your individual return at your individual tax rate. You report this business income on IRS Schedule C, *Profit and Loss From Business (Sole Proprietorship)*, which you file with your 1040 individual federal tax return.
Liability	As a sole proprietor, you're personally liable for all business debts and legal claims. Liability insurance may pay for some of your legal claims.
Formalities	A sole proprietorship is created automatically when you go into business. There is no fee to create one and no paperwork.

Can a Husband and Wife Be a Sole Proprietorship?

If spouses co-own and run a side business in a community property state (Arizona, California, Idaho, Nevada, New Mexico, Texas, Washington, and Wisconsin), they can operate as a sole proprietorship and report their business income as part of their joint tax return; or they can operate as a partnership and file a K-1 partnership return. If spouses co-own and run a business in a non-community property state, they must operate as a partnership and file a K-1 partnership return.

In all states, if one spouse owns the business and the other works for it, the business is a sole proprietorship, and the owner will have to declare the spouse as an employee or independent contractor. If the spouse occasionally volunteers to help the business without pay, you won't have to declare the spouse as an employee or independent contractor.

Partnership

If you're operating with others and haven't incorporated or formed an LLC, then you're a general partnership. (Limited partnerships are discussed in "Limited Partnerships and S Corporations.")

General Partnerships at a Glance	
Taxation	A general partnership is a pass-through tax entity. The profits (and losses) pass through the business entity to the partners, who pay taxes on any profits on their individual returns at their individual tax rates. Even though a partnership does not pay its own taxes, it must file an "informational" tax return, IRS Schedule K-1 (Form 1065). In addition, the partnership must give each partner a filled-in copy of this form showing the proportionate share of profits or losses that each partner reports on an individual 1040 tax return. A partner pays taxes on his or her entire share of profits, even if the partnership chooses to reinvest the profits in the business, rather than distributing them to the partners.
Liability	Each partner is personally liable for business debts and legal claims. The partnership should have liability insurance that will cover most claims. What's more, a creditor of the partnership can go after any general partner for the entire debt, regardless of that partner's ownership interest. Any partner may bind the entire partnership (in other words, the partners) to a contract or business deal.
Formalities	You don't have to pay any fees or prepare any paperwork to form a general partnership; you can start it with a handshake. It makes far more sense, however, to prepare a partnership agreement. (See "Partnerships: Get It in Writing," below.) You may want to hire an accountant to manage the annual tax returns and documents.

Partnerships: Get It in Writing

If you're going into a side business with someone as a partner, you should write a partnership agreement. Without an agreement, the one-size-fits-all rules of each state's general partnership laws will apply to your partnership. These provisions usually say that profits and losses of the business should be divided equally among the partners (or according to the partner's capital contributions in some states), and they impose a long list of other rules. You'll undoubtedly prefer to make your own rules. Your agreement should cover issues such as division of profits and losses, partnership draws (payments in lieu of salary), and the procedure for selling a partnership interest back to the partnership or to an outsider. *Form a Partnership*, by Denis Clifford and Ralph Warner (Nolo), explains how to form a partnership and create a partnership agreement.

If you're not comfortable preparing your own agreement, an attorney should be able to prepare one for between $500 and $1,000.

What's the Difference? LLC vs. Corporation

The LLC combines the best feature of corporations (limiting the owners' personal liability) without any changes in tax reporting (you file the same tax documents as sole proprietorships and partnerships). An LLC can be formed by one or more people. LLCs have largely replaced corporations as the favorite choice among small business owners and are discussed in more detail later in this chapter.

Corporations are the most formal of the business entities. Owners hold shares (becoming shareholders) and elect a board of directors that directs management. If you incorporate your small business, you become an employee but still run it. Corporations are distinguished for tax purposes, as "C" corporations or "S" corporations. A C corporation is a regular for-profit corporation taxed under normal corporate income tax rules. (When we use the term corporation in this book, we always mean a C corporation.) In contrast, S corporations are taxed like partnerships—their income is passed on to the owners.

Most start-up business owners prefer LLCs because reporting and paying individual income taxes is easier than the corporate alternative. If you switch from a sole proprietorship or general partnership to an LLC, there won't be any changes in how you do your income tax reporting. That's because, like sole proprietorships and partnerships, most LLCs are pass-through entities. Pass-through taxation means that you report the money you earned from your business on your individual tax return and pay tax at individual income tax rates.

A corporation is not a pass-through entity; it's taxed as a separate entity, at a corporate tax rate. When the corporate profits are passed to the owners, they are taxed again on individual returns.

As a business develops and income increases, however, some owners prefer corporate taxation because the owners of a corporation can split business income between themselves and their business so that some business profits are taxed at the lower corporate tax rate. Small corporations can also offer employees fringe benefits, such as fully deductible group life and disability insurance, enhanced retirement plans, stock options, and other incentive plans. The owner/employees of corporations are not taxed on their individual tax returns for these benefits.

Finally, don't assume that forming an LLC or a corporation will *always* shield all of your personal assets. Even if you operate as a corporation or an LLC, a creditor can still go after your personal assets if:

- You personally guarantee a loan or lease.
- You owe federal or state taxes.
- Your business is subject to potential negligence claims.
- You fail to abide by corporate rules—for example, you mix corporate and personal funds and don't keep records of meetings and shareholders. In that case, a judge may strip away the asset protection feature of the corporation or LLC. It's called "piercing the veil."

LLCs and Corporations at a Glance		
	LLC	**Corporation**
Taxation	An LLC is taxed like a partnership—or, for a one-owner LLC, as a sole proprietorship. Income, loss, credits, and deductions are reported on the individual tax returns of the LLC owners. The LLC itself pays no income tax.	A corporation is a legal entity separate from its shareholders. The corporation files its own tax return (IRS Form 1120) and pays its own income taxes on the profits kept in the company.
Liability	LLC owner/members aren't personally liable for business debts and other liabilities. However, they're liable for debts that they personally guaranteed and tax debts.	A corporation's owners (shareholders) aren't personally liable for business liabilities. However, they're liable for debts they personally guaranteed, tax debts, and claims based on their negligence.
Formalities	To start an LLC, you must file articles of organization with the state business filing office. You and the other owners should also prepare an operating agreement to spell out how the LLC will be owned, how profits and losses will be divided, how the interests of departing or deceased members will be bought out, and other essential ownership issues.	To form a corporation, you pay filing fees and file organizational papers, usually called articles of incorporation, with a state agency (most likely, the secretary or department of state). Directors must hold annual meetings and keep minutes, prepare formal documentation (resolutions or written consents to corporate actions) of important decisions made during the life of the corporation, and keep a paper trail of all legal and financial dealings between the corporation and its shareholders. The board of directors must appoint officers to supervise daily corporate business.

How to Convert to an LLC or a Corporation

As a sole proprietor or partnership, you can convert to an LLC in most states with a modest amount of paperwork and fees and with no change to your income tax treatment and filing requirements. Here are three ways you can handle the conversion:

- **Do it yourself.** You can learn more about incorporation or LLC formation procedures and fees for your state by visiting your state's business filing office website, usually the website of the secretary of state. (Start by finding your state's home page at www.statelocalgov.net, then look for links to business resources.) You can also get step-by-step instructions on forming an LLC in *Form Your Own Limited Liability Company*, or forming a corporation in *Incorporate Your Business: A Legal Guide to Forming a Corporation in Your State*, both by Anthony Mancuso (Nolo).

- **Hire an incorporation service.** Companies such as Nolo (www.nolo.com), the publisher of this book, will incorporate your business or form an LLC on your behalf, usually for $200 to $300 in addition to the regular filing fees. To locate one of these services, type "incorporation service" into your Internet search engine.

- **Hire an attorney.** An attorney can help form a corporation or an LLC, usually for a fixed fee between $500 and $1,000 (plus filing fees).

If you're a sole proprietor, you can convert your one-person side business to a corporation or an LLC or bring additional owners into the business when converting. You don't need to be a resident of the state where you form your LLC, or even of the United States, for that matter.

If you are a partnership, you and your partners must agree to terminate the partnership and convert to a corporation or an LLC. You may have to complete additional paperwork to legally terminate your partnership when you convert it to an LLC—for example, you may need to publish a notice of dissolution in a newspaper. Check with your secretary of state.

Finally, before you decide to convert to another entity, you should seek the advice of a tax consultant about possible tax consequences. You'll also want advice on the effects of having your new corporation or LLC assume the debts of your prior partnership.

By the way, don't forget about payroll taxes. For payroll tax purposes, an LLC owner who receives a share of the profits is not considered an employee. However, the owner who receives a salary—that is, guaranteed payments from the business, regardless of how much it earns—is an employee, and the LLC must withhold and pay income and other payroll taxes on the salary payout.

Limited Partnerships and S Corporations

Two types of business entities that have faded from favor in the last few decades are limited partnerships and S corporations.

A limited partnership has two types of partners: general partners who manage the business and limited partners who are typically investors and contribute capital to the business, but are not involved in day-to-day management. Only the limited partners have limited liability protection. General partners are personally liable for business debts and claims. The limited partnership is taxed like a general partnership, with all partners individually reporting and paying taxes on their share of the profits each year.

S corporations still exist, but, like limited partnerships, they have largely been replaced by LLCs. The S corporation's shareholders receive the same basic pass-through tax treatment afforded sole proprietorships, partnerships, and LLC owners. S corporation shareholders have limited personal liability for the debts and other liabilities of the corporation.

An Interview With LLC and Corporations Expert Anthony Mancuso

The following are excerpts from an interview with attorney Anthony Mancuso, who's a recognized expert on business formations and the author of such best-selling titles as *Incorporate Your Business*, *Form Your Own Limited Liability Company*, and *How to Form a Nonprofit Corporation* (Nolo).

QUESTION: Tony, when people find out that you've written all these books on business formation and corporations and LLCs, is there one common question that you're often asked?

ANTHONY MANCUSO: People usually ask a very general question— "What is the best form of business?"—when they hear that I write books for Nolo. I usually tell them the best form is no form at all until you have a reason to think about it. If you're worried about lawsuits, if you're going into business with someone else and want to make sure you have an agreement in place that covers some of the contingencies, then it might be time to start thinking about it.

Typically, once people worry about limited liability issues or take a look at insurance costs and worry about uninsured risks and those types of things, that's when they may think about forming an LLC, a limited liability company. When they want to raise capital, or find that they're making a little too much money and getting taxed on everything, then they may think of forming a corporation to shelter some money in their corporation. But generally, that's my answer: Wait until there's a need and it becomes important; wait till it's more than a theoretical question.

QUESTION: Is the LLC always the best choice for the owner of a start-up business seeking to limit personal liability?

ANTHONY MANCUSO: It generally is, although people who haven't heard the news about LLCs often think of S corporations. But really, the LLC has replaced the S corporation. The LLC lets you form a legal entity that insulates you from liability for business mistakes—that's claims against your business—and at the same time, it keeps your current tax status. So if you're a sole proprietor and you form a one-person LLC, you'll continue to be taxed as a sole proprietor. If you're a partnership and you convert to an LLC, you'll continue to have your business taxed as a partnership, so you don't change your tax status.

QUESTION: If you're trying to form an LLC or a corporation by yourself—that is, without the aid of an attorney—are there one or two things that you really need to watch out for?

ANTHONY MANCUSO: The first thing is to really stay focused on forming an LLC in your own state. If you go on the Web and you take a look at a number of the books, you may see a lot of talk and titles about forming a Delaware LLC or a Nevada LLC, or forming out of state where the taxes are lower. That doesn't do you much good. In fact, it just creates more problems. You want to stay in your home state because that's where you'll be taxed, ultimately. It won't matter if you form a Delaware corporation and you make your money in California—California is going to want to tax you anyway. So you won't save anything. In fact, you'll be setting yourself up for double costs if you do that.

So, stay within your own state. I would suggest if you know someone who's experienced with business taxes and law, it's always a good idea to have a consultation with them for an hour, just to make sure about your decision to form an LLC and the tax consequences. With LLCs, if they're co-owned, they're taxed as partnerships, and partnership taxation is quite complicated. There's a number of elections to think about ahead of time. So it's really a good idea, particularly from a tax perspective, to go over your decision to form an LLC with a tax person who really knows partnership taxation.

QUESTION: There's a lot of advice available for people who want to form an LLC or a corporation, but you don't see much discussion about what it takes to shut down one of these entities. How hard is it to dissolve an LLC or a corporation?

ANTHONY MANCUSO: Well, fortunately, most secretaries of state have online forms to do it. It's usually just a one-step process. At least, legally it's a one-step process. You'll file a dissolution form in most cases, with the state, and it'll dissolve it. It's a little more involved from a tax perspective because you usually have to get a tax clearance from your state tax agency, and that's simple enough. In some states, though, it's not quite as simple. In California, for instance, which has its own tax forms—(it doesn't follow the federal tax forms), you'll have to file a special tax form with the Franchise Tax Board. But you'll also need a tax clearance.

QUESTION: Tony, you hear lawyers talking about "piercing the corporate veil." What is it, and how often does it happen?

ANTHONY MANCUSO: Yeah, it's a really bad mixed metaphor, but it generally means that in some situations, the owners of a corporation or of an LLC can be held personally liable for the debts of the business or claims made against it. So, suppose someone sues your LLC or corporation, claiming you caused damage or injury. If they can convince a court to pierce the corporate veil, they can go after your personal assets as well. Of course, the main reason for forming an LLC or a corporation is to insulate yourself from those types of personal liabilities. When someone successfully pierces the veil, they've defeated the protection normally afforded by your incorporation or your LLC formation, and that's something you don't want to see happen.

It's very, very rare that courts allow the protection of the LLC or corporation to be disregarded, and that's the main thing to keep in mind. It only happens in cases where someone has committed a fairly serious fraud against someone else or acted without the authority of the corporation or LLC, and a court determines that the only fair way to resolve a dispute is to hold someone personally liable.

QUESTION: Do people really need to worry about personal liability if they have sufficient business insurance?

ANTHONY MANCUSO: If you feel comfortable with your current level of coverage, given the type of business you're in, then you don't really need to worry too much about your business form, at least for legal liability reasons. You may want to form a particular type of business for tax purposes. But the main reason to form an LLC or a corporation, for legal purposes, is to limit your liability. If you have adequate insurance—by the way, you're in the minority—but if you do, then maybe you don't have to think about it, and you can just go about your life and your business without worrying about this. But, for most people, that's not true.

If you're dealing with the public, if you have people coming onto your property, or if you're doing any kind of contract type of business with others, it's just true these days that disputes often end up in court or have the potential to. It helps business owners sleep better at night to have this type of automatic liability protection, which they obtain by incorporating or forming an LLC.

Insurance

When you're operating a small side business, money is usually tight— and you're probably reluctant to spend what little you have insuring against disasters that will probably never strike. On the other hand, it's foolish to do some side businesses without basic insurance coverage. What's more, you may be required to have some types of insurance by law or by those you do business with (lenders, landlords, and others).

The trick is to get only the coverage you really need—and to pay as little as possible for it. We'll explain the basics, below.

Basic Coverage

If you decide to get insurance for your side business, you'll be faced with a few choices. Here's a brief description of some common insurance protections.

Property Insurance

Business property insurance compensates you for damage to or loss of your property—both the physical space where you work (your home office, for example) and the equipment and other furnishings of your business. If you operate a home business, you can probably take care of your property insurance needs through an endorsement to your homeowners' policy, particularly if you don't have much pricey business equipment. But don't assume that your homeowners' policy will cover business losses—most offer very limited coverage (if any) for business property.

Key Insurance Terms	
Policy	Your policy is the written document or contract between you and the insurance company.
Premium	The premium is the periodic payment you pay to the insurance company for the benefits provided under the policy.
Rider	A rider is a special provision attached to a policy that either expands or restricts the policy.
Claim	A claim is your notification to an insurance company that you believe a payment for a loss is due to you under the terms of the policy.
Commission	This is a fee or percentage of the premium you pay to an insurance broker or agent.
Deductible	The deductible is the amount of out-of-pocket expenses that you must pay before the insurance payment begins. For example, if your deductible for business equipment loss is $1,000 per year and you suffer $1,000 in damages in one year, there will be no payment under the policy.
Endorsement	An endorsement is paperwork that is added to your policy and that reflects any changes or clarifications in the policy.
Exclusions	Exclusions are things your insurance policy will not cover.
Underwriter	This is the person or company that evaluates your business and determines what insurance you may qualify for.

If you rent commercial space—for example, a studio for your jewelry business—your lease may require you to carry a specified amount of property insurance.

A "named peril" policy protects against only the types of damage listed in the policy—typically, fire, lightning, vehicles, vandalism, storms, smoke, and sprinkler leaks. A "special form" policy offers broader coverage, commonly against all but a few excluded risks (often including earthquakes) and is more expensive.

When you're buying property insurance, you'll have a choice between an actual cash value policy, which pays you whatever your damaged property is actually worth on the day it is damaged, or a replacement cost policy, which pays to replace your property at current prices. A replacement cost policy is always more expensive, but it's often worth the extra money. Business equipment, such as computers, fax machines, copiers, and so on, lose their value quickly. And if you're like most new business owners, you're probably using some equipment that's already out of date. If you suffer a loss, you'll need to replace this equipment and get back to work—not to go out to a fancy lunch on the $100 your insurance company thinks your old computer was worth.

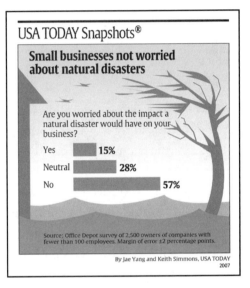

USA TODAY Snapshots®

Small businesses not worried about natural disasters

Are you worried about the impact a natural disaster would have on your business?

Yes 15%
Neutral 28%
No 57%

Source: Office Depot survey of 2,500 owners of companies with fewer than 100 employees. Margin of error ±2 percentage points.

By Jae Yang and Keith Simmons, USA TODAY 2007

Liability Insurance

Liability insurance covers injury to other people or damage to or loss of their property for which you are legally responsible. This includes, for example, injuries to a customer who trips on your son's skateboard on the way to your home office; damage caused by your products (called products liability coverage); and harm caused by your errors in providing professional services (called professional liability coverage). Liability insurance policies typically pay the injured person's medical bills and other out-of-pocket losses, any amount you are ordered to pay in a lawsuit for a covered claim, and often the cost of defending you in such a lawsuit. If you have a home business and are seldom visited there by clients or customers, you may be able to get a relatively inexpensive liability endorsement to your homeowners' policy.

Car Insurance

If you have a car, you probably already have insurance that covers your personal use. However, your personal insurance policy may not cover business use of your car. If it doesn't, you'll want to get business coverage to protect against lawsuits for damage you cause to others or their vehicles while using your car for business.

If you don't do much business driving—and particularly if you don't often have business passengers, such as clients or customers—then you can probably get coverage simply by informing your insurance company of your planned business use (and paying a slightly higher premium). Many insurance companies simply factor in occasional business use of a vehicle, along with commuting miles, driver experience, and many other factors, in setting your insurance premium. If you use a commercial vehicle (such as a van or delivery truck) or put most of the miles on your car while doing business, you will probably have to get a separate business vehicle insurance policy.

Business Interruption Coverage

If your side business becomes your primary source of income, we recommend that you obtain business interruption insurance—a policy that replaces the income you won't be able to earn if you must close, rebuild, or relocate your business due to a covered event, such as a fire or storm. These policies typically provide both money to replace your lost profits, based on your business's earnings history (as shown by its financial records), and money to pay the operating expenses you still have to pay even though you can't do business (like rent and overhead). If you are not dependent on your side business, you may not wish to spend money on this type of policy.

When you're shopping for this type of insurance (or any other, for that matter), always check the exclusions and coverage. For example, some policies may provide an "extended period of indemnity," which kicks in after you reopen, to cover your continuing losses until you are fully back on your feet. If your customers don't immediately flock back to your new location, your policy will pay for the business you're still not getting during this transition period.

USA TODAY Snapshots®

Crime may not pay, but it costs

Estimated value lost by victims of property crimes[1] in 2005 (in billions):

Motor vehicle thefts	$7.6
Larceny-thefts	$5.2
Burglaries	$3.7

Source: U.S. Department of Justice   1 – excludes arsons

By David Stuckey and Adrienne Lewis, USA TODAY 2006

Web Insurance

Some insurance companies offer Web insurance policies, which protect businesses with websites against a variety of risks, including theft, copyright infringement, and interruptions of service. Today, you can get insurance for a simple site for anywhere from $500 to $3,000 a year. An insurance professional can help you decide whether your cyber-risks are great enough to justify this expense.

Malpractice Insurance

Anyone who sells professional services (those that require advanced education or training) could conceivably be sued for harming someone by providing services that don't meet the standards of the profession. For example, a masseuse whose poor technique injures a client or a website creator who delivers a site that is immediately hacked could face a claim for professional negligence, often referred to as malpractice. Of course, the fact that you can be sued for something doesn't necessarily mean you should insure against it. And because malpractice insurance is often expensive, you may want to assess the chances of a lawsuit from a disgruntled client before paying for this type of policy.

Package Deals

Many insurance companies offer package policies geared to the needs of small businesses. If you run a home business, you may be able to get less expensive coverage through an in-home business policy. These policies typically cover business property and liability, and some also provide business interruption protection. According to the Insurance Information Institute, an in-home business policy will cost something in the range of $250 to $400 a year for about $10,000 of coverage. However, your business will have to meet the insurance company's requirements for coverage, which may include having no more than a very few employees, bringing few business visitors to your home, or purchasing your homeowners' insurance from the same company.

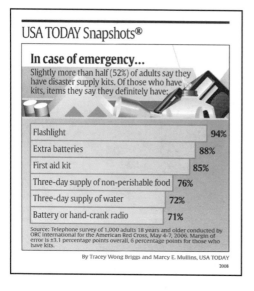

USA TODAY Snapshots®

In case of emergency...
Slightly more than half (52%) of adults say they have disaster supply kits. Of those who have kits, items they say they definitely have:

Flashlight	94%
Extra batteries	88%
First aid kit	85%
Three-day supply of non-perishable food	76%
Three-day supply of water	72%
Battery or hand-crank radio	71%

Source: Telephone survey of 1,000 adults 18 years and older conducted by ORC International for the American Red Cross, May 4-7, 2006. Margin of error is ±3.1 percentage points overall, 6 percentage points for those who have kits.

By Tracey Wong Briggs and Marcy E. Mullins, USA TODAY 2008

If your home business can't meet these requirements, or if you run a business outside of your home, you can consider a business owners' policy or BOP. These packages typically include business property insurance, liability protection, and some business interruption protection. According to Chad Berberich, director of Executive Products at RLI Corporation Insurance (www.rlicorp.com), a "mom and pop" home-based business with revenues up to the low six figures can expect to pay an annual premium of anywhere from $1,500 to $4,000 for a BOP.

Typically, neither a BOP nor an in-home business policy provides coverage for professional liability (malpractice), employment practices liability (often referred to as EPLI) to protect you from lawsuits brought by current or former employees, workers' compensation, or other employee benefits (health or disability insurance, for example). Also, you will almost certainly have to pay separately for automobile coverage if you use your car for business.

Insurance for Employees

Do you have any employees? Keep in mind that when you hire employees, you take on some financial obligations. In addition to paying wages and Social Security and Medicare taxes for each employee, you'll also have to pay for unemployment insurance and, in a handful of states, disability insurance. And if you have more than a few employees, you'll probably have to purchase workers' compensation insurance.

USA TODAY Snapshots®

Unsafe at work
Number of workplace safety and health violations found:

83,539 ('03–'04 range)   88,846

90,000
60,000
30,000
0
'03   '04   '05   '06   '07

Source: Occupational Safety & Health Administration
By David Stuckey and Alejandro Gonzalez, USA TODAY
2008

If you have formed an LLC or corporation and you list yourself as employee (and even if you don't have employees), you may have to pay for workers' comp insurance to cover your own work-related injuries. This rule may vary from state—for example some states only require workers compensation coverage once you have a total of three employees. Here's a more detailed description of the types of insurance you will need:

- **Workers' compensation insurance.** This insurance pays your employees for work-related injuries and reimburses them a portion of lost wages if they cannot work due to injury. You buy it either by paying into a state fund or by buying a policy from a private insurer. Some states don't require employers that have only a few employees to get this coverage; contact your state insurance or labor department to find out your state's rules.

- **Unemployment insurance.** If you have even one employee, you will probably have to pay for unemployment insurance (UI). UI is a joint program of the state and federal governments. It's funded by a payroll tax on employers, which goes into a fund from which workers who are laid off or fired for reasons other than serious misconduct can draw money while they're unemployed. The amount you have to pay will depend on how many employees you have and how many unemployment claims your former employees have made (if any). For information, go to the website of the federal Department of Labor's Employment and Training Administration, at www.doleta.gov. Choose "Business & Industry" for a list of topics for employers, including UI.

Don't Count on Customers' Liability Waivers

If you're in a high-risk business (for example, you offer rock-climbing clinics), you might think you can shift some risk to your customers by asking them to sign liability waivers, which are agreements that they are responsible for their own safety and cannot sue you if they are injured as a result of your negligence. Your insurance pro may advise you to ask clients to sign these waivers as a first line of defense. However, if a dispute arises over who's responsible for a serious injury, you should be prepared for the possibility that a court might throw out the agreement. In other words, these waivers don't always work. Because of legal rules that limit how far people can go to dodge responsibility for their own carelessness or wrongdoing, such waivers are often difficult to enforce. Any attempt to absolve yourself from extreme, or "gross" negligence, will most certainly be thrown out by a court.

- **Disability insurance.** Five states (California, Hawaii, New Jersey, New York, and Rhode Island) provide temporary disability insurance to workers who are temporarily disabled and unable to work. In California and Rhode Island, employees pay the cost of this insurance through payroll deductions; in Hawaii, New Jersey, and New York, employers pay into the plan. If you do business in one of these states, go to your state labor department's website to find out more about your obligations.

Ten Tips for Saving Money on Insurance

Besides keeping your coverage up to date—be sure to set aside a time once a year to consider whether you need to increase your coverage—there are many ways to make sure you're not wasting money on insurance. Here are ten tips.

Insurance Tip #1: Get Group Insurance Through an Association

If you belong to a trade organization, professional group, or other business association, you may be eligible for special rates on certain types of insurance. For example, if you become a member of the National Association for the Self-Employed (www.nase.org), your business may be entitled to insurance discounts for your home office. Every field of business has membership organizations, and some of them may provide specialized or group insurance plans. For example, the Association of Pet Dog Trainers (www.apdt.com) offers members access to group liability insurance policies, and the American Institute of Certified Public Accountants (www.aicpa.org) makes a variety of insurance programs available to its members. If you practice acupuncture and are in the market for malpractice insurance, group rates are available through the American Association of Oriental Medicine, www.aaom.org.

Insurance Tip #2: Work With the Right Insurance Professional

Try to find someone who will help you figure out what coverage you need and offer you a competitive price. There's no magic formula for finding the "right" insurance professional. You need to find someone whom you trust to do a good job for you, and who will periodically provide you with information about new policies you might want to consider, give you quotes from other companies from time to time, and help you if you have to file a claim.

Insurance Tip #3: Use Your Client's Insurance

In some business fields, your clients may have to provide the insurance. For example, Mike and Carrie McAllen, who run Grass Shack Events & Media (www.grassshackroad.com), a company that plans events mostly for corporate clients, find that their clients often supply the insurance for their events. Many of their events are held in hotels and similar facilities. Because the client books the venue, Mike says, it is the client who has to show proof of adequate insurance for the event. (In a situation like this, be sure that you have been named as an "additional insured" on the client's policy.) Of course, this doesn't meet all of Grass Shack's business insurance needs, but it helps lower the bills.

Insurance Tip #4: Start Saving for Required Insurance

If you are legally required to carry certain types of insurance (such as workers' compensation), make sure you set aside the money for it.

Insurance Tip #5: Prioritize Your Greatest Risks

Once you've dealt with required coverage, spend your money where you need it the most. If you face a serious risk of a loss that could wipe you out, put your insurance dollars there first.

Insurance Tip #6: Consider Higher Deductibles

When you purchase a policy with a higher deductible, you'll pay lower premiums. This can be a financial lifesaver if you need insurance and you're struggling to get off the ground.

Insurance Tip #7: Don't Duplicate the Coverage You Already Have

Take time to review your homeowners' or renters' insurance policy to determine whether you already have coverage that may protect you for your side-business activity.

Insurance Tip #8: Consider Riders to Your Existing Policies

Home-based businesses that have few business-related visitors can get a relatively inexpensive liability endorsement (a document that modifies the policy). You can also add an endorsement to increase coverage for business equipment. If you use your personal car for business and your existing auto insurance policy doesn't cover business use, you may be able to get the coverage you need through an endorsement. However, if you use a car solely for business, you'll have to buy a separate business/commercial auto policy.

USA TODAY Snapshots®

Biggest computer security concerns

What types of computer security issues does your organization face? Top responses:

Virus/worm — 70%
Lack of user awareness — 60%
Abuse by authorized users — 46%
Remote access — 45%
Browser-based attacks — 40%

Note: Multiple responses allowed
Source: CompTIA's Fourth Annual Benchmark Study, Committing to Security survey of 2,598 information technology professionals. Margin of error ±2 percentage points.

By Jae Yang and Julie Snider, USA TODAY 2006

Insurance Tip #9: Always Read the Fine Print

Before you write your premium check, make sure you understand exactly what you're getting for your money. Check the terms, exclusions (what isn't covered), limits, and so on.

Insurance Tip #10: Make Sure You Can Collect if You Need to

If you need to make an insurance claim, you'll have to prove the extent of your loss. For property, you should photograph and keep records of the value of your business equipment, inventory, and so on. If you have very valuable items (the type of valuables that will be excluded from a policy unless you obtain an endorsement), consider having them valued by an independent appraiser.

Insurance Resources

- The Insurance Information Institute, www.iii.org, offers lots of free information on insurance and a glossary of common insurance terms.
- The Federal Small Business Administration offers a free primer on business risk and ways to transfer that risk (including insurance) at www.sba.gov. Type "business risk" into the site's search box.
- Insure.com offers extensive insurance information for small businesses, at http://info.insure.com/business. Be sure to check out the "Small Business Liability Tool" (under "Small Business Insurance Tools"), which allows you to choose a profession, from gun shop owner to Web designer, then view common risks and recommended types of insurance.

Reduce Your Risks

Aside from incorporating or obtaining insurance, there is one final (and free) step you can take to reduce your personal liability: Assess and lower your business risks.

Assess Your True Risks

By assessing your risks, you can determine if you need to be concerned. Assessment can also guide you as to how much protection is needed. Answer the following questions:

- **How much business property do you own?** The more you own, the greater your loss in the event of a setback or disaster.
- **Do you sell products?** If so, what are the chances that they might cause someone injury?

- **Do you carry a large inventory of completed products or valuable raw materials?** The larger your inventory, the more of a financial loss from damage. If your raw materials are hazardous, you may face additional risks.

- **If you sell services, could a client suffer harm (physical or financial) if you made a mistake?** If so, you may want to consider malpractice insurance.

- **Will you have employees?** Employees increase your risks and liabilities.

- **Are you a target?** The wealthier you are, the more likely you will appear as a target for those who might want to file a claim against you or sue you.

Reduce Your Risk

Minimize your risks. Doing so may eliminate your need to form a separate business entity and it may bring your premiums down.

Consider your list of possible risks (above) and think about what you can do to eliminate them or reduce the potential for danger. Sometimes risk prevention requires investigation, like learning about customers, suppliers, and people you employ. Sometimes, it's just a matter of common sense—if you're a ski instructor, be sure you have a selection of helmets for students who have forgotten to bring their own.

USA TODAY Snapshots®

When is information on paper most at risk?

In a trash bin **62%**

In a communal printing tray **46%**

At an office desk **44%**

Awaiting disposal or shredding **31%**

Note: Multiple responses allowed

Source: Alliance for Secure Business Information survey of 819 workers. Margin of error ±4 percentage points

By Jae Yang and Veronica Salazar, USA TODAY 2008

You can transfer risk to others, as well. For example, don't store a lot of supplies or finished products on your premises, but leave them at your rented studio space. (Of course, this strategy will work only if the person or company where you store things is adequately insured.)

Avoid the Lawyers

Lawyers are not your enemy … but they can be expensive friends. They provide invaluable, sometimes crucial, advice but if you're operating on a shoestring, you probably can't afford the hourly rates (usually over $250). Fortunately, often you don't really need an attorney.

In this chapter, we'll focus on a few of the areas where a lawyer's guidance is sometimes needed—for example, when drafting contracts, choosing a business name, and protecting business ideas—and we'll provide ways to save money in the event you need to bring in the legal team. You may be surprised how much you can manage on your own.

Ten Common Contract Problems and How to Solve Them

The phone rings. It's a client or customer and they've got a great proposal for all. The deal sounds good and then they speak those dreaded words: "Could you put together a contract for me?" Preparing a contract can cause concern. After all, contracts bind your business (or you), they're written in legalese, and they sometimes contain unexpected legal landmines. Here are ten of the most common contract problems and how to deal with them.

Problem #1: You Don't Know Anything About the Other Party

Keep in mind the advice of William Burroughs, who once said that "paranoia means having all the facts." A contract, no matter how carefully drafted, cannot insulate you from a liar or a cheat. In other words, it isn't always what's on the paper; it's who is signing it. Therefore, if you have any doubts, the most important and easiest way to avoid contract problems is to investigate the other side. There are a lot of ways to do that.

You can ask for references and also perform a basic Internet search and check news articles. (Search engines, such as Google, have a "News" link that will search newspaper articles.) Be on the lookout for items about lawsuits, financial problems, or any unusual business dealings. Consult the Better Business Bureau to see if there are complaints against the firm, or use one of the Internet business reporting websites such as www. hoovers.com or www.dnb.com. If you're still unsure after doing your research, go with your gut instinct.

USA TODAY Snapshots®

Becoming a lawyer
Overall passage rates of bar examination:

70%   65%   64%

1996   2000   2005

Source: National Conference of Bar Examiners

By David Stuckey and Alejandro Gonzalez, USA TODAY
2007

Problem #2: You Didn't Get It in Writing

Oral agreements have obvious advantages—simplicity, efficiency, and a sense of trust. But the uncertainty and vagueness of oral deals leaves the door wide open for protracted disputes in which the wealthier party always has an inherent advantage. For that reason, we recommend that you always "get paper," as they say in the music business—that is, get it in writing. If you do enter into an oral agreement, preserve any documentation—from letters to cocktail napkins—whatever it is that details the key features of the deal, and if possible, write a letter confirming your understanding.

Problem #3: You Want to Dispute a Contract But You Can't Afford to Hire a Lawyer

One way to even the playing field is to think ahead and to insert an attorney fees provision in the contract. That way, in the event of a legal dispute over your contract, the attorney fees provision establishes that the loser will pay the winner's legal fees. This provision can be especially helpful in preventing pyrrhic victories—where the fees exceed the damages. Typically, an attorney fees provision is one sentence and it reads something like, "In any dispute arising under or related to this agreement, the prevailing party shall have the right to collect from the other party its reasonable costs and attorney fees."

Problem #4: You're Not Sure That The Other Side Is Accounting to You Properly

Let's say your contract has to do with sales and you're pretty sure the accounting statements are off. If you had inserted an audit provision, you could examine the other side's books in the event of an accounting dispute. Avoid a provision that requires you to bring only a certified public accountant to an audit. CPAs are expensive, and you may prefer to bring your non-CPA accountant.

Problem #5: Payments Are Continually Late and You Want to Terminate (But the Agreement Is for One Year)

Either party can terminate an agreement if the other party commits a material breach—that is, a major breakdown of the agreement. But late payments may not always qualify as a material breach. The solution is to include a termination provision that specifically defines material breaches as including a failure to make timely payments.

Problem #6: A Third Party Sues Both Parties to the Contract (Even Though You Didn't Do Anything Wrong)

Let's say you have a contract to maintain exercise equipment at a gym. Somebody is injured at the gym, and even though the accident has nothing to do with your maintenance, you are named in the lawsuit. There's not much you can do about being named in the lawsuit, but there is a way to specify who will pay for your legal fees and court costs. In your contract, you can add a provision called an indemnity, or "hold harmless," provision, which means that if you end up with fees and costs arising out of an incident that you were not responsible for, the other party will cover your expenses. A clause like this can work for you or against you, because usually one runs both ways—if the gym, for example, incurred costs because you had, in fact, negligently repaired their equipment, you would have to reimburse them. Because these clauses are tricky, it's a good idea to always read them carefully and if in doubt, check with a lawyer. In particular, avoid indemnity provisions that are overly broad (you don't want to end up paying for the other side's fees and costs over a trivial matter—this simply encourages litigation in place of compromise or settlement). Stay away from a provision that indemnifies the other party for any breach of the agreement.

Problem #7: You Want to Go After the Other Party to the Contract But They Are Located in Another State

This is a complex subject and let's just say that your chances of recovery are much better if the contract specifies which state's law governs disputes (ideally, your state). More importantly, your contract should require that the other party consent to being sued in your state—sometimes known as agreeing to your state's "jurisdiction." The jurisdiction clause is also known as a forum selection clause. With such a clause, if you or the other party file a lawsuit arising under the contract, you'll each have to file it in the agreed-upon court in your state.

It's often difficult to get a jurisdiction clause that's to your advantage because, of course, the other side wants just the opposite (that their state's laws will apply, and any lawsuit will be brought in their state, not yours). We bring this up not just in the hopes that you will be able to get a favorable clause, but also so that you'll be aware of it in case the other side tries to bind you to appear in their state. Two states, Idaho and Montana, refuse to honor these provisions and other states have required that the parties have some contact with the state beyond the contract provision—for example, they must do business with the state's citizens.

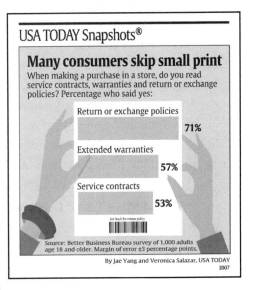

USA TODAY Snapshots®

Many consumers skip small print

When making a purchase in a store, do you read service contracts, warranties and return or exchange policies? Percentage who said yes:

Return or exchange policies — 71%

Extended warranties — 57%

Service contracts — 53%

See back for return policy

Source: Better Business Bureau survey of 1,000 adults age 18 and older. Margin of error ±3 percentage points.

By Jae Yang and Veronica Salazar, USA TODAY 2007

Problem # 8: You're Supposed to Provide the Agreement But You Can't Afford to Hire an Attorney and You're Not Sure How to Write a Contract

Start with the concept that lawyers don't actually write contracts from scratch—they build them around existing templates or borrow pieces from other form agreements. You can do the same. We suggest that you start with a good form agreement. Thanks to the do-it-yourself legal movement, there are many quality agreements to choose from. We advise you, however, not to make your decision solely based on price. Every bargain software bin contains a *1,000 Legal Forms* disk and most of them are not reliable. Instead, look for a company that regularly updates its products with new editions, update notification services, and so forth and that provides explanations for all the provisions in the agreement. Also, if you are part of any industry or guild, check out their offerings. Professional and trade organizations such as the American Institute of Architects (AIA), the Graphics Artist Guild (GAG), and the American Trucking Association (ATA) provide standardized, high-quality contract documents for members. (By the way, Nolo (the publisher of this book) has one of the best form–agreement products available. It's *Quicken Legal Business Pro*.)

Problem # 9: You Can't Understand the Boilerplate

Boilerplate is the term used to describe standard provisions usually found at the end of most agreements. They are created by lawyers to deal with odd and uncommon contingencies. Here's a rundown on what a few of these provisions mean.

- An **entire agreement** provision (sometimes referred to as the "integration" provision) establishes that the agreement is the final version and that any modification must be in writing. It prevents parties from later claiming, "But you told me such-and-such."

- If you include a **waiver** provision, neither side can claim that the other set a precedent by deviating from the agreement in some way—for example, accepting payment later than usual. ("But you didn't object when I was late before, so that changed the terms of the deal.")

- A **severability** provision (aka invalidity provision) permits a court to sever (take out) a portion of the agreement that's no good while keeping the rest of the agreement intact. In this way, one legal error in a contract won't torpedo the whole transaction.

- A **force majeure** provision allows you or the other side to not perform as required under the agreement if doing so is rendered impossible or highly impractical by a supervening event over which you had no control—for example, a fire destroys your business. The clause is sometimes referred to as the "act of God" clause.

Problem #10: You're in a Hurry to Do the Contract and You Don't Want the Formality of Written Agreements

Use an electronic agreement. Electronic contracts and signatures are as legally valid as paper contracts, thanks to a federal law enacted in 2000. An electronic contract (or e-contract) is just an agreement created and "signed" in digital form—for example, through an exchange of emails. For example, you write a contract on your computer and email it to a business associate, who emails it back with an acceptance ("I accept this"). An e-contract can also be in the form of a "click to agree" contract (the user clicks an "I agree" button). Although electronic agreements are binding, like oral agreements, you can enforce them only if you have proof of the contract. So always keep records, either a digital backup or a printout of these electronic transactions.

Drafting and Formatting an Agreement

In the event you are drafting your own agreement, here are some suggestions.

Avoid legalese. Using legalese—uncommon phrases and wording that seem like a secret language—can make your agreement ambiguous.

Instead of "whereas" and "heretofore," use words with common and everyday meanings. Set out each party's rights and obligations in as clear a manner as possible.

Don't contract for something illegal. Just because both parties agree on something doesn't mean a court will enforce the agreement. Contracts that violate laws or public policy will not be enforced—for example, an agreement to charge an illegal interest rate or to conspire to limit commerce unfairly. By the way, you can find each state's legal interest rate at Virgin Money (www.virginmoneyus.com). Choose "Business Loans," then click "More Tips & Tools."

Be specific. To create a legally enforceable agreement, you must agree on the material terms, which are the important things people bargain for—the who, what, how much, how many, where, and when questions. Having a written agreement isn't, by itself, enough to make it enforceable. For example, the widow of the novelist John Cheever had a written agreement with a publisher to publish a collection of his stories, but the contract didn't specify the content of the book, and it didn't establish when the manuscript was to be delivered, when the book would be published, or what would happen if the book were no longer in print. When Mrs. Cheever didn't cooperate with the publisher, it sued to force her. The court would not enforce the contract because it lacked essential terms. (*Academy Chicago Publishers v. Cheever*, 144 Ill. 2d 24, 578 N.E.2d 981 (1991).)

Anticipate problems. Lawyers earn big bucks for anticipating contract disasters and providing a means—ahead of time—of resolving them. Focus on the most likely and most damaging potential problems. For example, what happens if goods aren't delivered on time? Will you provide a period to correct the problem? How (and where) will you resolve disputes? And be sure to anticipate the biggest problem—the other side is untrustworthy (more on that later).

Use standard provisions. There is common ground in every written agreement, regardless of the specifics of the deal. It's usually in the form of the standard contract clauses discussed later in this chapter. If you understand these commonly used provisions, you're on your way to understanding most contracts.

Pay attention to appearance. Whether it's a letter agreement or a 30-page license, the look of your contract matters. True, there's no law that says your contract must look like it came from a lawyer. But your contracts should reflect a professionalism that instills trust. Number the contract provisions, provide boldfaced titles, and use a clear, formal font.

Who Signs the Agreement?

Only someone with the necessary authority can sign an agreement for the following types of businesses:

- **Sole proprietor.** You sign, of course, and you're personally liable.
- **Partnership.** Any general partner or person given authority by a general partner can sign. All of the owners will be personally liable for the obligations under the agreement unless the agreement excludes them from liability.
- **Corporation or LLC.** Only a person authorized by the business can sign contracts—usually the president, CEO, or an executive. The name of the corporation or LLC should appear above the signature line, and the name and title of the person signing should be included below the signature line. The signing party for a corporation or an LLC won't be personally liable unless the agreement says so.

When You Have to Review a Contract

Lawyers believe that you're more likely to get what you want if you write the first draft of the contract. For that reason (or simply because the other side likes to use its own familiar agreement), a company or individual may give you their contract to use. Reviewing someone else's agreement is the flip side of writing one. Be prepared to spend an hour or two making your analysis. Here are some suggestions on how to proceed.

Step 1. Read

Make a photocopy of the agreement and read it through. If you can understand everything, great—you may not need an attorney. If you can't understand something, flag the confusing provision or section.

Step 2. Compare

Compare the agreement either to similar ones you've signed in the past or to a form agreement. Look for glaring differences—for example, their agreement says that the photographer owns the copyright, while your agreement says that the client owns the copyright.

Step 3. Prepare

Prepare a table listing the number of any section you want modified and explaining your concerns and the changes you want made—for example, add a new provision, strike this section, and so forth. You can later convert this table into a response letter to the other side or you can use it as the starting point for talking with an attorney.

Test Your Legalese

Sometimes the biggest challenge when reading a contract is sorting through the jargon. Here's a test of your knowledge of legalese. Can you match the term with the meaning?

Term	Meaning
1. herein	a. previously
2. hereinafter	b. considered as
3. heretofore	c. in spite of
4. notwithstanding	d. from this point on
5. foregoing	e. in this document
6. deemed	f. preceding

Answers: 1e, 2d, 3a, 4c, 5f, 6b

Maintaining Paperwork

Maintaining your contracts is an essential element of your business record keeping. Your contract files should contain, in addition to the signed contract:

- correspondence and copies of email regarding the contract
- drafts with changes made by the parties (this will help to show what you intended, if there's ever a disagreement), and
- whatever documentation exists, especially in the case of oral contracts, to prove the existence of the agreement—receipts, notes, and, if possible, your own memo to the file detailing the terms.

Are You Afraid of Negotiating Contracts?

Many books teach how to negotiate a contract, but most people agree that the classic *Getting to Yes*, by Roger Fisher and William Ury (Houghton Mifflin), is the best of the bunch. Fisher and Ury emphasize:

- separating the people from the issues (removing the emotion)
- looking beyond the negotiating parties to see who or what is the real interest or influence affecting each party
- generating options to create a problem-solving environment, and
- neutralizing conflict by sticking to objective and easy-to-justify principles of fairness.

If you're new to business and negotiation, you may be stuck for the right things to say while discussing a deal. Try creating scripts ahead of time. Below, (in the right-hand column) are examples of how to use five "magic phrases" gathered by writer Jenna Glatzer ("Those Magic Phrases—How to Negotiate Like a Pro," *Home Business*, Sept. 1, 2004). The left-hand column indicates what you might actually be thinking.

Negotiating Like a Pro	
You think	**You say**
That's ridiculous. I can't believe they're even offering that.	That sounds a little low.
There's no way I can do that work at that price. My hourly rate would be a joke.	To make it worth my time, I would need at least …
They're being completely unrealistic. Their offer doesn't even include the cost of goods.	Considering the amount of __ required, can we agree to …
They must be used to dealing with low-quality outfits and they're obviously not familiar with my standards.	I'm expecting more for this work.
There's absolutely no hope for this deal.	Can we work on that?

Avoiding Legal Problems With Names and Trademarks

Even the tiniest side business has a trademark. It is the name (or logo or other signifier) that consumers see when purchasing your products and services. (If you sell services, it's technically a service mark, but for our purposes we'll refer to both as trademarks.) A business can have many trademarks.

Your legal name is the name you use when communicating with the government or other businesses—that is, it's the name you use to buy property, file tax returns, and write checks. You must get clearance for your legal name from your state government as part of the incorporation or LLC formation process. State government clearance is not required for sole proprietorships or partnerships, though they often must file fictitious business name documents with a county government office. This clearance has nothing to do with your right to use your name as a trade name or trademark, as described below. For example, getting corporate clearance for your business name will not shield you from trademark disputes from another company with a similar name.

Choosing a name similar to that of a competitor often triggers disputes. And if the competitor's been using the name longer than you have, you'll lose the battle of the names. A similar name is one that is likely to confuse consumers—for example, you see a camera named "Cannon" and think it is a Canon. To create a legal problem, the similar name must be used on similar goods or services.

Determining the degree of similarity is part science and part witchcraft, and sometimes depends on the sophistication of the consumers. If you're in doubt as to whether a name you are choosing is too similar, put yourself in the competitor's shoes and look at the choice from that perspective. Would you feel ripped off?

Perform a Simple "Knockout" Search

You cannot register or use a trademark that's confusingly similar to an existing trademark used in a similar class of goods or services as yours. You should search the U.S. Patent and Trademark Office (USPTO) trademark database (www.uspto.gov) when changing or choosing a new name. Look for current and pending trademark registrations using the USPTO's TESS (Trademark Electronic Search System) database.

To access the database at www.uspto.gov, click "Search" under "Trademarks." If your search yields a mark that you think conflicts with your mark, check its status via the USPTO's TARR system (Trademark Applications and Registrations Retrieval) database. Many trademarks in the database are abandoned or "dead" and should not pose a problem for your application. This type of search (called a knockout search) will uncover the most obvious marks similar to yours. Attorneys traditionally recommend that you follow this up with a professional trademark search as provided by companies such as Thomson & Thomson (www.thomson-thomson.com).

Don't assume you get any trademark rights by creating a clever name. You don't get legal rights because you create a name. You get rights only when you use the name in commerce. You can reserve name rights with the federal government—and we'll explain how later in this chapter— but these rights don't exist until you use the mark in commerce.

Federally Registering a Trademark

Should you file a federal trademark application? Even without register-ing, you still have rights under state laws. You can always stop someone with a similar name from competing in your area for similar products or services, provided you can prove you used the name first. Always keep in mind that name rights are awarded because you were the first to use the name in com-merce in connection with those products or services.

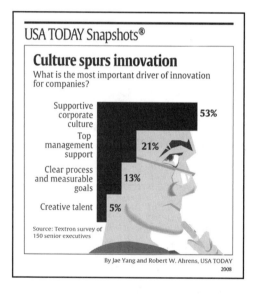

USA TODAY Snapshots®

Culture spurs innovation
What is the most important driver of innovation for companies?

Supportive corporate culture — 53%
Top management support — 21%
Clear process and measurable goals — 13%
Creative talent — 5%

Source: Textron survey of 150 senior executives

By Jae Yang and Robert W. Ahrens, USA TODAY
2008

And having a federal registra-tion does not automatically prevent someone from using a similar name. You will still have to pay an attorney to chase those who infringe on your trademark.

Consider filing a federal trademark application if you consistently sell products or services across state lines or plan to expand nationally. Registering a trademark with the USPTO makes it easier for the owner to protect it against would-be infringers and puts the rest of the country on notice that the mark is already taken.

The registration process involves filling out a simple application and paying an application fee ($325 per class of goods, if filing electronically using TEAS, the Trademark Electronic Application System). Nolo (www.nolo.com), the publisher of this book, also offers an online trademark application program

However you file, you must also be prepared to work with an official of the USPTO to correct any errors in the application. To qualify a mark for registration with the USPTO, the mark's owner first must put it into use "in commerce that Congress may regulate."

This means that the mark must be used on a product or service that crosses state, national, or territorial lines—for example, a catalog or Internet business that sells products to customers in different states, or a restaurant or motel that caters to interstate or international consumers.

If you're not yet using the mark in commerce, you can file an intent-to-use application, which is used when the applicant intends to use the mark in the near future but hasn't yet begun using it. If you file an intent-to-use application, another document—a statement indicating your actual use of the mark—must be filed later, along with an additional fee once the actual use of the trademark begins. And you must show the USPTO that the mark is now being used in commerce.

Once the USPTO receives your trademark application, it determines the answers to these questions:

- Does the application have to be amended (because of errors)?
- Is the mark the same as or similar to an existing mark used on similar or related goods or services?
- Is the mark on a list of prohibited or reserved names?
- Is the mark generic—that is, does the mark describe the product or service itself rather than its source?
- Is the mark descriptive—that is, does it consist of words or images that are ordinary or that literally describe one or more aspects of the underlying goods or services?

Once you satisfactorily provide the answers to these questions to the USPTO, the agency will publish the mark in the *Official Gazette* (an online publication of the U.S. Patent and Trademark Office) as being a candidate for registration.

Existing trademark and service mark owners may object to your registration by filing an opposition. If this occurs, the USPTO will schedule a hearing to resolve the dispute.

If there is no opposition, and use in commerce has been established, the USPTO will place the mark on the list of trademarks known as the Principal Register.

Probably the most important benefit of placing a mark on the Principal Register is that anybody who later initiates use of the same or a confusingly similar mark will be presumed by the courts to be a "willful infringer" and, therefore, liable for any losses or injuries you suffer as result of their unauthorized use of your trademark.

The federal registration lasts for ten years. During that time, you have certain obligations to maintain your trademark registration—for example, you must file a Section 8 Declaration of Continued Use form between the fifth and sixth anniversaries of the registration. You can find information about the registration procedure as well as the maintenance requirements at the USPTO website (www.uspto.gov). For more on trademark registration procedures, check *Trademark: Legal Care for Your Business & Product Name*, by Stephen Elias and Richard Stim (Nolo).

Staying Out of Trademark Trouble

You've probably read about disputes in which one company sues another over its trademark. Or maybe you've heard about a big company pushing around a smaller business—as might happen, for example, if McDonalds wanted to stop a company from using "McSushi" or "McSoup." Do you need to worry about a dispute over your business name?

Probably not. It's estimated that fewer than 4,000 lawsuits are filed each year in federal courts over trademark issues. And many of these lawsuits aren't even about the right to use a name. They're about the abuse of names by counterfeiters or by consumers.

Even if someone does hassle you over your name, chances are good that you can resolve the dispute efficiently with a few letters or a call to a lawyer. For most small business owners, the odds of getting a letter from an attorney about a business name are slim to none.

When it comes to using another company's trademarks, here are a few suggestions that will help you stay out of legal trouble.

Don't mislead consumers when selling reconditioned goods. A company customized Rolex watches by replacing internal elements and adding diamonds. The company sold these as Rolex watches, and the Rolex company sued to stop the sales. The court ruled that because the reconditioning was so severe, it was unfair to call the watches Rolex. (*Rolex Watch U.S.A., Inc. v. Michel Co.*, 50 USPQ 2d 1939 (9th Cir. 1999).)

Don't assume you can use trademarks from ratings or awards. Most companies that provide ratings or give awards provide guidelines for the use of their marks in advertising. Some require written permission; some, like Consumers Union, publisher of *Consumer Reports*, prohibit any use of their trademark in advertisements.

Don't advertise trademarked ingredients without permission. If you sell homemade candy featuring Grand Marnier brand liquor, don't give undue prominence to this (or any other) trademarked ingredient. For example, avoid saying "Intel Inside" if you assemble computers, unless you meet the conditions for use of the Intel trademark posted at the Intel website.

Trademark Symbols

Typically, the symbols®, TM, or SM are used with trademarks—for example, IBM® or Happy Boy Music Store™. The symbol® indicates that a trademark has been registered with the USPTO; it is illegal to use this symbol if the trademark has no USPTO registration. If your trademark or service mark hasn't been federally registered, you can use the TM symbol or SM symbol. The TM and SM have no legal significance, but indicate that the owner is claiming trademark rights.

Don't confuse the source when selling complementary or add-on products. The Apple iPod has spawned an industry of products that complement the popular player, such as amplifiers, recording devices, and holders. It's okay to state you're selling an iPod holder, for example, but don't create the impression that it's endorsed or sold by Apple.

Don't mislead consumers on the Internet. There are many ways for a business to mislead consumers on the Web, and new ones keep popping up. For example, ShoesforSale.com puts the name of a competitor, Zappos.com, in its website code (in a form known as a metatag). When a consumer searches for Zappos, ShoesforSale.com turns up in the search results. The courts have not consistently resolved how to deal with these issues, but regardless of whether you will win or lose in court, you still face the costs of defending yourself in a dispute.

Don't assume you can sell trademark parodies. Sometimes it's permissible to parody a trademark. Parody is imitation that pokes fun at the mark—for example, by selling caps printed with the words, "Mutant of Omaha." But offensive parodies are likely to trigger lawsuits. For example, lawsuits were filed over lewd photos of the Pillsbury doughboy and of nude Barbie dolls. Although the artist in the case involving Barbie dolls eventually won his claim, it required substantial legal effort and expense. (*Mattel Inc. v. Walking Mountain Productions, Inc.*, 2001 U.S. App. LEXIS 2610 (9th Cir. 2002).) A trademark parody is less likely to run into problems if it doesn't compete with the trademarked goods and services and doesn't confuse consumers—that is, they get the joke and do not believe the parody product comes from the same source as the trademarked goods.

Four Steps to Legally Protecting Your Business Ideas

The secret to success of many businesses is to have ideas that others cannot copy. These are known as proprietary ideas because they are the exclusive property of the business, which can stop competitors from using them. When we speak of business ideas, we are referring to products of the mind—innovations and creative thinking that we associate with inventions, new processes, books, artwork, crafts, or similar creative products. If your business plans on exploiting these kinds of ideas, you'll be looking to seek the maximum legal protection in the form of a copyright, patent, trademark, or trade secret. As you can see from the steps below, the key to protecting ideas is recording them accurately and knowing your rights.

Step 1. Record Your Ideas

This may seem obvious, but we'll say it anyway: Having an idea is never enough. No matter how you come up with your business idea—while exercising, driving, or perhaps standing in the shower—you can't protect it unless you have expressed it in a manner that can be judged,

USA TODAY Snapshots®

Most employers don't share company strategy

Of the companies with a formal strategy in place, 70% describe their performance as better than their competition, compared with 27% of those without it, according to a survey. Percentage of companies that tell their employees what the strategy is:

Don't tell **95%**

Tell **5%**

Source: Cognos/Palladium Group "Making Strategy Execution a Competitive Advantage" study of 143 strategy management professionals.

By Jae Yang and Alejandro Gonzalez, USA TODAY 2006

recorded, and registered. In the case of books, art, and music, it's simply a matter of recording your work—for example, putting your image on canvas or your words on paper. In the case of a patentable invention, you must explain your idea with a written description that clearly explains how to make and use your invention or, alternatively, create a working prototype. For example, you may have an idea for improving pizza delivery boxes. But unless you can express that idea in a manner that meets the standards of patent protection, your idea will have little value. That makes sense under the law, because without this fixed expression or manifestation of your idea, it would be difficult for the government to offer protection, provide systems of registration, or resolve disputes.

Step 2. Identify What's Proprietary

You need to determine if you have any "Rembrandts in the attic," as one popular book on business ideas puts it. "What Ideas Do You Have?" below, points you toward the things that qualify as proprietary and protectable.

Step 3. Ensure Your Rights

Register your valuable ideas with the agencies that oversee copyrights, patents, and trademarks. If you have trade secrets, take steps to maintain the confidentiality of the information. We explain the basics later in this chapter.

Step 4. Enforce Your Rights

Perhaps an ex-employee has taken your customer list; maybe a competitor is imitating your trademark in order to siphon customers. Going after these people (infringers) can be expensive and disappointing—for example, you may win a lawsuit only to learn that the infringer has closed up shop and disappeared. We'll offer you some tips on when to pursue infringers and when it's not worth the effort.

What Ideas Do You Have?

You can't protect your ideas unless you can categorize them. Lawyers refer to this process as an intellectual property audit (protectable expressions of ideas are referred to as intellectual property or IP). An IP audit is often performed before the sale of a business. Like any audit, you create an inventory, and as new IP is created, licensed, or acquired, you add that to the inventory.

Here are some questions to help you uncover your IP:

Have you developed new products, formulas, recipes, technologies, or processes? Functional devices, technologies, formulas, or processes that were invented by your business within the past few years may be protected under trade secret or patent law.

Does your business create original works, such as crafts, music, artwork, film, or publications? Artistic and/or creative products or publications are protected under copyright law. Copyright even extends to some unexpected places—for example, software programming and architecture. Some art may also be protected under design patent law—for example, furniture, jewelry, or toy designs.

Have you created business plans, financial projections, marketing plans, sales data, or similar strategy directives? The results of your business strategy brainstorming sessions are protected under trade secret law, provided you keep them confidential.

Have you created new ways of doing business? You can get a patent (sometimes referred to as a business method patent) on a way of doing business. For example, Netflix, the online movie rental service, has a patent on its "method and apparatus for renting items" that covers the process used for its subscription service.

Have you prepared a website, advertising, or marketing or promotional materials? Promotional efforts like websites and advertisements are usually protected under copyright law.

Have you created names and logos to identify your business, products, or services? The ways in which the public identifies your products and services—commercial signifiers like names, logos, and choice of color schemes—are protected under trademark law.

Do you have customer lists or other industry database information? You might not think of a database or customer list as something you can stop others from using, but under certain conditions, described below, they can be protected under trade secret law. A customer list is more likely to qualify as a trade secret if the information in the list is not easily ascertainable by other means and if the list includes more than names and addresses—for example, pricing and special needs.

Ensuring Rights: Registration and Other Measures

With the exception of trade secrets, if you plan to enforce your rights in your IP, you'll have to file some papers with the federal government. Here's the scoop.

Copyright

Copyright protection begins once a work is created and generally lasts for the life of the creator plus 70 years. Works made for hire (discussed below) are protected for 120 years from their date of creation or 95 years from their first publication, whichever is longer. If you want to sue an infringer, you'll need a copyright registration.

USA TODAY Snapshots®

Inventive minds want to know about copyrights
Internet hits to key U.S. Copyright Office Web pages:

(in millions)

12 '01 13 '02 16 '03 20 '04 29.5 '05

Source: United States Copyright Office

By David Stuckey and Alejandro Gonzalez, USA TODAY
2006

We recommend using the U.S. Copyright Office website (www.copyright.gov), where you can download copyright application forms or copyright publications that explain copyright laws and rules in plain language. For additional help, check Nolo's copyright resources and products at www.nolo.com. The filing fee for registration is currently $45 ($35, if filing electronically), and the registration process takes approximately six months. If you have to do it in a hurry—for example, you want to file a lawsuit—you can expedite the registration for an added fee (more than $500). If you can't afford to register all of your copyrighted works, register your most popular items—that is, the ones most likely to be copied.

Utility Patents

Obtaining a patent is a time-consuming process that can be quite expensive—often costing more than $10,000. Be sure you have cleared a few hurdles before you consider it.

The first hurdle is to check whether a similar invention or method already exists. You can do a basic search of patent records on the Internet at the USPTO website (www.uspto.gov). Nolo's *Patent Pending in 24 Hours*, by Richard Stim and David Pressman, and *Patent Searching Made Easy*, by David Hitchcock, explain how to do basic searches.

The second hurdle is to determine whether your idea is marketable. For several hundred dollars, you can perform your own marketability studies—for example, by interviewing potential customers, retailers, or distributors to gauge interest in your product. A few universities evaluate inventions for inventors at a very reasonable price—for example, the WIN Innovation Institute (www.innovation-institute. com), affiliated with Southwest Missouri State University charges approximately $250 to determine how probable it is that your invention will be accepted in the marketplace.

The third hurdle is to verify your invention's novelty by paying for a professional patent search. This search will give you a more realistic idea than your basic search as to whether previous inventions or publications (known as prior art) will prevent you from getting a patent. You can locate patent searchers over the Internet or find one through a patent lawyer. A professional search will cost $300 to $1,000.

If you're wary of this whole process, but want to preserve your place at the USPTO for one year, you can file a document known as a provisional patent application. It's not expensive (less than $100) and once you've filed, you can claim your invention as "patent pending" and test it in the market before seeking a patent. For more on provisional patent applications, use Nolo's online filing procedure or read *Patent Pending in 24 Hours*.

If you decide to apply for a utility patent, you can pay a professional or learn how to file the application yourself. For some people, the expense of hiring a patent attorney is the biggest barrier. If your funds are limited (or if you just can't stand the idea of paying an attorney), consider doing it yourself—or doing as much as you can and then bringing it to an attorney to review or help. You may well want help with the most important and difficult to draft section, the claims. The claims set the boundaries for what's protected by the patent.

Once you get a patent, you may exclude others from making, using, or selling the patented subject matter throughout the United States for 20 years from the filing date of the patent application. In reality, this means a patent lasts for approximately 17 to 18 years because it takes the USPTO—the agency that oversees patents—a few years to examine and approve the application.

Design Patents

Design patents protect new and "nonobvious" ornamentation of a useful object, from the flickering icon on your computer screen to the shape of your MP3 player. Preparing and filing a design patent is fairly simple—especially compared to preparing and filing a utility patent. If you're a self-starter with a do-it-yourself mindset, you can, with a bit of work, prepare your own design patent application and save anywhere from $500 to $1,000 in lawyer's fees. A design patent lasts for 14 years.

"Protection" May Not Really Protect You

Once you have a copyright, trademark, trade secret, or patent, you're protected, right? Wrong. You're protected only if you're willing to sue people who use your ideas without permission. Considering that lawsuits over these issues commonly cost $50,000 or more in attorney fees (and there's no guarantee that you'll get it back), it's no wonder that many people find it too expensive to enforce their rights.

Trademarks

If you want to stop others from using your name, logo, or some other commercial signifier, register your trademark at the USPTO. We discuss trademarks earlier in this chapter in "Federally Registering Your Trademark."

Trade Secrets

Trade secrets consist of any information that is known by you but not your competitors. If you have trade secrets (not all businesses do), the law allows your business to protect that material as long as you take reasonable precautions to keep the information confidential. In general, a business is considered to have taken reasonable steps if it uses a sensible system for protecting information—for example, by locking its facilities, monitoring visitors, and labeling confidential information. A crucial part of your company's trade secret maintenance should be to require contractors, employees, investors, and others exposed to confidential information to sign a nondisclosure agreement (NDA). A person who reveals or misuses your protected information after signing a nondisclosure agreement can land in serious legal trouble. You can not only seek a court order barring further disclosure or misuse of your information, but you can sue for financial damages as well.

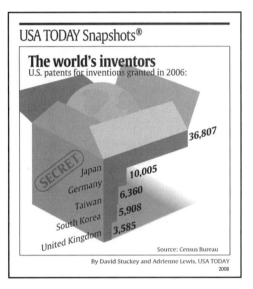

USA TODAY Snapshots®

The world's inventors
U.S. patents for inventions granted in 2006:

36,807

Japan 10,005
Germany 6,360
Taiwan 5,908
South Korea 3,585
United Kingdom

Source: Census Bureau

By David Stuckey and Adrienne Lewis, USA TODAY 2008

Asking contractors to sign an NDA may seem burdensome or out of character. But the American Society of Industrial Security estimates that U.S. businesses lose at least $24 billion a year because of stolen trade secrets, most of it from the transfer of secrets by employees. Using a nondisclosure agreement may prove to be the most effective method of protecting your side business and its confidential information. For free copies of nondisclosure agreements and more on trade secrets, check out www.ndasforfree.com.

Chasing People Who Rip Off Your Ideas

If someone rips off your trade secrets, copies your copyrighted or patented work, or steals your trademark, you can make them stop and perhaps get compensated for the damage they've done. Not every dispute over ideas ends fairly or happily. Edwin H. Armstrong, the man who pioneered and patented modern radio communications, claimed that RCA and other communication companies had stolen his innovations. Eventually, he was so beaten down by the decades of litigation that he jumped to his death. It wasn't until 32 years after his patents had been granted that his widow eventually settled the cases with RCA, Motorola, and Emerson.

On the other hand, not every dispute turns into a lawsuit. Sometimes, a letter from your lawyer, along with evidence of registration of your trademark, copyright, or patent, will be enough to halt the infringement. In other cases, you may have to file a lawsuit and hope for a quick settlement. Your attorney can advise you on litigation—but beware that some attorneys are eager for litigation simply because they can make a lot of money from it. Proceed cautiously before filing a lawsuit. Here are some things to consider.

Most people don't get rich over infringement lawsuits. With the exception of egregious patent or copyright thefts, you're unlikely to earn a windfall by winning an infringement lawsuit. Usually, you're awarded the infringer's profits (or your lost profits) and not much else. In many cases, the costs of the lawsuit exceed the amount recovered.

Most people don't get awarded attorneys fees. The judge will order the losing party to pay your attorney's fees only if the infringer acted willfully or intentionally. This excludes many, many infringers who were unaware they were infringing or who stopped once notified of the infringement.

You risk losing your rights. Infringers commonly argue that the patent, copyright, or trademark at issue is invalid, or that the information wasn't a trade secret. If the infringer proves invalidity—for example, someone invented your device before you filed your patent—your golden goose will be dead.

Investigate the financial stability of the person you're suing. It's foolish to sue someone who can't pay or who will disappear into cyberspace. And, generally, avoid filing a lawsuit unless the infringement is likely to affect your bottom line.

Avoid filing lawsuits solely based "on principle." Attorneys love clients who fight on principle. That means the battle will continue much longer than when the client's decisions are based on business realities— for example, that it's cheaper to settle than litigate. This isn't to say you should abandon your ethical principles; just don't let this be the primary motivator for filing a suit.

Licensing or Selling Your Rights

You can make money selling your rights to someone else, either temporarily (a license) or permanently (an assignment). In return for letting a company use proprietary rights, you earn a percentage of the revenue generated (a royalty). For example, the artists who created Cabbage Patch dolls earned millions from licensing their creation. Similarly, Ray Dolby's company was built upon licensing its noise reduction patents to audio manufacturers.

What If You Copy Somebody Else's Ideas?

It's possible that someone may accuse your company of stealing ideas. The opening salvo in these disputes is usually a letter from an attorney demanding that you "cease and desist" from any further uses. To minimize any potential damages, you should:

- respond immediately, saying you received the letter and are investigating the claims
- investigate the claims and, if necessary, request further information from the owner of rights, such as proof of ownership
- if possible, stop using or distributing the device or work (for example, remove the photo from a website or stop selling a book) until the claim has been fully investigated, and
- contact an attorney knowledgeable in intellectual property law.

Not all legal threats are valid, so you will need an attorney's opinion. Be sure to ask your attorney for an estimate of the legal expenses for fighting the dispute.

Don't assume that you can use portions of a work on the basis of "fair use," a copyright principle that permits you to copy small portions of a work for purposes such as parody, scholarship, or commentary. In one case, a company published a book of trivia questions about the events and characters of the *Seinfeld* television series. The company believed it had a fair use right to include questions based upon events and characters in 84 episodes and used dialogue from the show in 41 of the book's questions. A court ruled it was not a fair use; the company had to stop publishing the book and pay financial damages. (*Castle Rock Entertainment, Inc. v. Carol Publ. Group*, 150 F.3d 132 (2d Cir. 1998).)

Ideas Created by Your Employees or Contractors

Who owns the ideas created by your workers? That depends on whether the worker is classified as an independent contractor or employee. Here are some basic principles:

- You automatically own everything—patents, trade secrets, and copyrights—created by employees in the course of their employment. Even so, it's preferable to have written agreements stating this with employees, particularly in the case of patents and trade secrets.

- You do not own things created by an independent contractor unless you both agree to it in writing. These agreements usually transfer ownership to you (known as assignments), although in the case of a copyright, your business may acquire ownership from an independent contractor under a principle known as a "work made for hire."

- An employee or independent contractor can never own the rights to your trademarks. The owner is always the business that first uses that trademark in commerce, regardless of who created it. However, if the trademark involves artistic elements (other than choice of font), it may be separately copyrightable, and an independent contractor may own rights under copyright law.

What's a Release and When Do You Need One?

If you want to use someone's name or image for business purposes, you may need a signed release. A release is a contract in which someone forgoes a right to sue you. Without it, the person might be able to bring you into court for various violations of personal rights.

Whether you need to obtain a release depends on why you want to use a person's name or image. If your use is for commercial purposes—for example, using a person's photo in an advertisement—always get a release. When in doubt, we recommend that you obtain a signed release. It is best to keep the release as short and simple as possible. That's because most people asked to sign a release do so on short notice and often balk if it is complex or intimidating.

Ten Ways to Save on Legal Fees

You may have heard the joke about the new client who asked the lawyer, "How much do you charge?"

"I charge $200 to answer three questions," replied the lawyer.

"Isn't that a bit steep?"

"Yes," said the lawyer. "What's your third question?"

As the joke indicates, it's important to get a clear understanding about how fees will be computed when you hire a lawyer. Here are three tried-and-true ways to save money on legal fees.

Money Saver #1: Hire the Right Attorney

The novelist Robert Smith-Surtees said there are three sorts of lawyers: able, unable, and lamentable. The biggest waste of time and money occurs when you need to ditch one lamentable attorney and hire another able one. When hiring an attorney, try to find one who seems interested in your side business and either already knows a lot about your field or who seems genuinely eager to learn more about it. Avoid the lawyer who's aloof and doesn't want to get involved in learning the nitty-gritty details of what you do. Avoid hypercautious nitpickers who get unnecessarily bogged down in legal minutiae. Look for a lawyer who blends sound legal advice with a practical approach—someone who figures out a way to do something, not one who offers reasons why it can't be done.

Money Saver #2: Save Money When You Meet with Your Attorney

Group together your legal affairs. You'll save money if you consult with your business lawyer on several matters at one time. For example, in a one-hour conference, you may be able to review the annual updating of your corporate record book, renew your Web hosting agreement, and check over a noncompetition agreement you've drafted for new employees to sign. Also, help out. You can do a lot of work yourself.

Help gather documents needed for a transaction. Write the first couple of drafts of a contract, then give your lawyer the relatively inexpensive task of reviewing and polishing the document. And when working on a contract with an attorney, avoid spending too much time on negotiations. Lawyer's fees can quickly get out of control if negotiations for contracts drag on too long. Contracts sometimes go through many drafts. As long as you and your attorney are conscientious, you can get away with fewer drafts. Make sure you and the attorney are in agreement as to the goals of the contract negotiation. Tell your lawyer your priorities. Once you have achieved most or all of your goals, be flexible about the remaining issues so that you can save time.

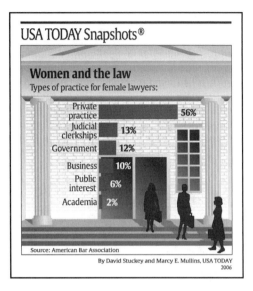

USA TODAY Snapshots®

Women and the law
Types of practice for female lawyers:

Private practice	56%
Judicial clerkships	13%
Government	12%
Business	10%
Public interest	6%
Academia	2%

Source: American Bar Association

By David Stuckey and Marcy E. Mullins, USA TODAY 2006

Money Saver #3: Try for Flat Fee Agreements (and Get Your Fee Agreement in Writing)

And as you bring new tasks to the lawyer, ask specifically about the charges for each. Many lawyers initiate fee discussions, but others forget or are shy about doing so. Bring up the subject yourself. Insist that the ground rules be clearly established.

When hiring a business attorney, you may be able to obtain a fixed, or flat fee for certain transactional work. That's ideal because flat fees give your business some predictability; you're not waiting for a billing surprise at the end of the month. And get your fee agreement in writing. In California, all fee agreements between lawyers and clients must be in writing if the expected fee is $1,000 or more, or is contingent on the outcome of a lawsuit. In any state, it's a good idea to put your fee agreement in writing.

Money Saver #4: If You Must Litigate, Be Realistic

When you hire an attorney because you're in the midst of a dispute, you're seeking someone who can defend your turf against others who threaten your side business. But don't assume you need the biggest ape in the jungle. Sometimes, a shrewd negotiator or a logical, methodical attorney can be the ideal choice to end a dispute amicably.

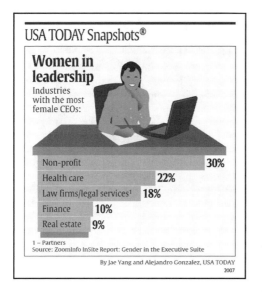

USA TODAY Snapshots®

Women in leadership
Industries with the most female CEOs:

Non-profit	30%
Health care	22%
Law firms/legal services[1]	18%
Finance	10%
Real estate	9%

1 – Partners
Source: ZoomInfo InSite Report: Gender in the Executive Suite

By Jae Yang and Alejandro Gonzalez, USA TODAY
2007

Whoever you hire, avoid lawsuits that go on forever. Litigation often costs $10,000 or more and the people who profit are the lawyers. If you're in a dispute, before screaming "I'll see you in court!" ask your attorney for a realistic assessment of your odds for success and the potential costs. The assessment and underlying reasoning should be in plain English. If a lawyer can't explain your situation clearly to you, he or she won't be able to explain it clearly to a judge or jury. Also ask your attorney about alternative dispute resolution methods, such as arbitration and mediation (see "Use Meditation or Arbitration," below). Always be skeptical of an attorney who assures you of a large windfall.

Finally, encourage settlement. A settlement is a contract signed by both parties, usually executed at the time one party pays the other. A negotiated settlement saves money (litigation costs) and time (you avoid waiting three years for the case to end). Better still, it results in a guaranteed payment (unlike a court judgment that you have to collect). These advantages create an incentive for you to accept less money in settlement than you would demand in a court case. When deciding whether to accept a settlement, you and your lawyer should consider your likelihood of winning in court and estimate any resulting award of damages if you were to lose.

Money Saver #5: Don't Fall for Attorney Advertisements or Lists of Lawyers Provided by a Local Bar Association

Advertisements found in the yellow pages, in newspapers, on television, or most online sites say nothing meaningful about a lawyers' skills or manners—just that they could afford to pay for the ad. Similarly, local bar associations often maintain and advertise lawyer referral services. However, a lawyer can usually get on this list simply by volunteering. Very little (if any) screening is done to find out whether the lawyers are any good. For a site that does give you extensive information, however—such as the lawyers education, background, fees, areas of expertise, and practice philosophy, check out Nolo's Lawyer Directory at www.nolo.com.

Money Saver #6: Keep Your Phone Calls Short

If you are paying your attorney on an hourly basis, keep your conversations short—the meter is always running. Avoid making several calls a day. Instead, consolidate your questions and ask them all in one conversation.

Money Saver #7: Review Billings Carefully

Your lawyer's bill should be clear. Do not accept summary billings, such as the single phrase "litigation work" used to explain a block of time for which you are billed a great deal of money. And watch out for hidden expenses. Find out what expenses you must cover. Watch out if your attorney wants to bill for services such as word processing or administrative services. This means you will be paying the secretary's salary. Also beware of fax and copying charges. Some firms charge clients per page for incoming and outgoing faxes—and the per page cost can be artificially high.

Money Saver #8: Educate Yourself

Learn as much as you can about your matter and the related law. It's easy using legal research tools at websites such as Justia.com, Findlaw. com, and Nolo.com. These sites will help you keep up with specific legal developments that your lawyer may have missed. Send pertinent articles to your lawyer—this can dramatically reduce legal research time—and encourage your lawyer to do the same for you.

Money Saver #9: Use Small Claims Court

Using small claims court instead of a regular trial court is always a bargain, because it offers a lawyer-free environment where you can quickly settle most common monetary and contractual disputes (think *Judge Judy*). Small claims courts will accept cases worth up to a certain amount of money—the limits range from $2,500 to $25,000—but most state limits are between $5,000 and $10,000. As long as the amount you are seeking is below the limit (and the court has jurisdiction over the other party), you can file in your local small claims court. If the amount you are seeking is higher, you can reduce your claim (and give up on the difference) in order to take the case to small claims court. Nolo (www.nolo.com) has a small claims court center at its website that provides information about each state's limits as well as suggestions on how to proceed in court.

Money Saver #10: Use Mediation or Arbitration

Mediation and arbitration are referred to as alternative dispute resolution or ADR. These methods are often cheaper and faster than a lawsuit. If you and the other party in the dispute agree, you can proceed with either or both methods.

If you choose mediation, then a mediator will try to help you settle your dispute. "Try" is the key word here, because the mediator can't make a decision or bind the parties. Many states offer community- or court-based mediation designed to help parties arrive at their own compromise settlement with the help of a neutral third party. Mediation works best where the parties have an interest in staying on good terms, as is generally the case with neighbors, family members, or small business owners who have done business together for many years. This type of dispute resolution can be remarkably successful. For more information, see Nolo's Mediation Resource Center.

Arbitration is more decisive. It allows the parties to avoid a lawsuit and instead hire one or more arbitrators—professionals trained to evaluate disputes—to rule on a dispute.

Both methods have drawbacks. Mediation works only if both parties have a good faith desire to resolve their problems. Arbitration, unlike a court ruling, is not appealable (that's why it's called binding arbitration) and can be set aside by a judge only if the arbitrator was biased or the ruling violated public policy. Also, arbitrators must be paid, and their fees may run $10,000 or more. Finally, participants in arbitration often hire attorneys, so you may not avoid having to pay legal fees—though it is almost always less expensive than litigation.

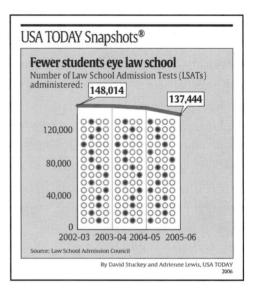

USA TODAY Snapshots®

Fewer students eye law school
Number of Law School Admission Tests (LSATs) administered:

148,014 ... 137,444

120,000 / 80,000 / 40,000 / 0

2002-03 2003-04 2004-05 2005-06

Source: Law School Admission Council

By David Stuckey and Adrienne Lewis, USA TODAY 2006

If you want to guarantee that these ADR procedures are used in the event of a contract dispute, you will need to include a mediation or arbitration provision in your agreement.

Evaluate Your Attorney's Services

How do you know if your lawyer is doing a good job? Generally, you can assume there is a problem if your attorney is not returning phone calls within 48 hours, the bills you're receiving are disproportionate to what the attorney predicted and there is no adequate explanation, or you are unable to understand why your attorney is doing certain things. It's never a good sign when your attorney speaks down to you.

As a general rule, if you leave the lawyer's office confused or unclear as to your course of action, there is a problem. After all, the primary job of an attorney is to counsel you as to your legal options. If you don't understand these options, the attorney has failed. This doesn't mean that the lawyer will always present a black-and-white explanation. There are many gray areas in the law. For example, the law regarding business names is often murky. A good attorney will explain this murkiness and evaluate your chances of success if a dispute arises over the use of your intended name. A good attorney will also provide you with accurate and understandable advice, permit you to make an informed decision as to how to proceed, and will work with you to efficiently resolve conflicts and solve problems. ●

Licenses, Permits, and Other Paperwork

E ven the smallest side business can't legally fly beneath the government's radar. For example, in the city of San Francisco, fortune-tellers have to post their rates, get fingerprinted, offer customers a written receipt, and get a fortune-telling permit from the city's police department. Although the San Francisco measure was billed as a way to protect consumers from charlatans, the real reason seems clear—it's a way to fill the city coffers. The city controller's office estimates that the city could net more than $46,000 annually if the estimated 130 fortune-tellers pay the permit fee.

As you can see, no matter what kind of side business you run, you'll have to register with—and perhaps pay fees to—the federal, state, and local governments where you do business.

For most of us, these registration requirements are easy to meet. You just fill out a few simple forms. However, while the paperwork is pretty straightforward, it's not always obvious exactly what you have to file and with which government agency. This chapter will help you cut through the red tape and get the licenses you need to run your business legally.

Basic Registration Requirements

Most businesses have to file a few standard forms with the federal, state, or local government. They include the following.

IRS Form SS-4, *Application for Employer Identification Number*

Despite its name, this form is required not only for businesses with employees, but for many businesses that don't have employees. An employer identification number (EIN) is a nine-digit number, like an individual's Social Security number, that's used by the federal government, to identify your business for tax purposes.

Your business must have an EIN if you have at least one employee. Even if you have no employees, you must get an EIN if:

- You have a partnership, limited liability company, or corporation (the EIN is necessary to identify your business on your tax returns).

- You are a sole proprietor and have a Keogh retirement plan (a plan for self-employed people), you buy or inherit an existing business, or you file for bankruptcy.

FINDING THE FORMS

The IRS has made it very easy to apply for an EIN. You can download Form SS-4 from the IRS website, www.irs.gov, then mail or fax it to the IRS. If you want to speed things along, you can complete your form online and submit it electronically (follow the instructions at the IRS website), or provide the required information to an IRS representative over the phone (800-829-4933). If you file electronically or by phone, you will immediately receive a provisional EIN, which will become your permanent EIN once the IRS verifies your application information. Don't forget to write the number down and store it someplace safe; if you file online, print a copy of the form for your records.

State Business License

A few states require any business within their borders to get a general business license. However, it's much more common for a state to require only certain types of businesses to get a license. If you work in a field that requires specialized training (engineering, nursing, or child care, for example) or deals extensively with consumers (such as home repair or tax preparation), you are likely to need a state license.

USA TODAY Snapshots®

What adults say is their idea of the American Dream

Free to accomplish anything — 74%

Free to say/do what they want — 68%

Children financially better off — 64%

Being financially secure — 61%

Note: Percentage rating these 8–10 on a 10-point scale, in which 10 is the perfect definition
Source: Pew Charitable Trusts survey of 2,119 adults Jan. 27–Feb. 8

By Anne R. Carey and Sam Ward, USA TODAY
2009

If you must get a license, expect to pay a fee and submit proof that you have the necessary education, training, or work experience. Fees range widely—in California, for example, a manicurist must pay an initial fee of $36, then a renewal fee of $41; if you want to train guide dogs, however, you'll have to pony up $250 at the outset, then pay another $100 every year. Depending on your field, you may also have to take a test, post a bond, allow the state to fingerprint you, show proof of insurance, or meet other requirements.

FINDING THE FORMS
To find out whether you have to get a state business license, go to your state's website. You can find a link to it at State and Local Government on the Net, www.statelocalgov.net; also check out the list of links to state Web pages that offer business license information at the website of the federal Small Business Administration, www.sba.gov/hotlist/license.html. Many state websites have small business centers online (these often have "one-stop" in their title) or links to state agencies and publications that deal with business matters.

Local Business License

Many cities and counties require those who do business within their limits to file a registration form. This form may be called a tax registration certificate, business license, business tax application, or something similar. No matter what the form is called, its purpose is the same: to tax your business. You may have to pay a flat fee or a rate that depends on your annual revenue. If your business is very small (as measured by its revenues), you may be exempt from a city or county licensing requirement.

FINDING THE FORMS
If you do business in a city, contact your city government to find out about licensing requirements and the necessary forms. If you do business in an unincorporated area, contact your county government. Many local governments have websites, and some post information for small businesses and post their forms online. You can find a comprehensive list of links to online local government agencies

at State and Local Government on the Net, www.statelocalgov.net. If you're looking for county ordinances online, go to the website of the National Association of Counties, www.naco.org. Click the tab "About Counties." Then you'll be able to search county codes and ordinances or look for a link to your county's website.

Don't Blow Off Zoning Requirements

When you register for a local business license, your local government will almost certainly check to make sure that your business meets the zoning requirements for the address you provide for your business. If your business isn't in compliance—because it's industrial in an area zoned residential, or it has too many employees, or because it will attract too much traffic, for example—you won't get a license. What's more, you can probably expect a city or county inspector to drop by and start issuing citations (or perhaps even shut you down) in fairly short order.

That's what happened to small business owners in Oakland, California. Using state tax records, the city of Oakland uncovered plenty of small businesses—many of them home based—that had not applied for city business licenses or paid local business taxes. In 2004, these business owners were hit with demands for back taxes and penalties going back to 2001.

Register Your Fictitious Business Name

If you do business under a fictitious name (often called a DBA, for "doing business as"), you probably have to register that name with your state or county government. A fictitious name doesn't refer only to a completely made up moniker, like Xerox or Kodak. Any name that doesn't precisely match your corporate, partnership, or limited liability company name is considered fictitious. And if you're a sole proprietor, any name that doesn't include your last name (or in some states, your full legal name) or seems to suggest that other people are involved in your business (such as John Brown & Associates), is fictitious.

In most places, you register a DBA with your county government. You will probably have to file a registration certificate (along with a fee, of course) with the county. You may also have to run a statement in a local newspaper for a set period of time, stating your DBA and your true name.

USA TODAY Snapshots®

Days it takes to start a business
How many days it takes to complete all requirements necessary to start a business in various countries:

Australia	2	
Canada	3	
USA	5	
South Africa	38	
Vietnam	56	
Brazil	152	
Haiti	203	

Source: The World Bank

By Shannon Reilly and Keith Simmons, USA TODAY
2005

The state wants you to register your name so it can track you down if your business does something wrong, such as ripping off consumers or skipping out on loans or bills. But there's plenty in it for you, too. For starters, registering your DBA puts other companies on notice that the name is taken—and stakes your claim to use the name as of the date you registered.

There are also some practical reasons to register your name. For example, some banks won't let you open a business bank account under your fictitious name unless you show them a registration certificate. And you may not be able to enforce a contract you signed using your business name unless you can show that you registered it properly.

FINDING THE FORMS
For information on registering a fictitious name, go to your county clerk's website. You can probably find a link to it at State and Local Government on the Net, www.statelocalgov.net. If you can't find the information you need there, check your state's website.

If You Sell Goods, Get a Seller's Permit

In most states, if you're selling goods, you need a permit from the state authorizing you to make sales and collect sales tax from customers within the state. Sometimes, the permit lets you buy items from wholesalers (for resale to customers) without paying sales tax. Some states call this a seller's permit; others call it a resale permit or something similar. (Note: You might need a permit even if your state doesn't have a sales tax. Even in the handful of states that don't impose a sales tax—Alaska, Delaware, Montana, New Hampshire, and Oregon—local governments sometimes impose sales taxes, which you may be required to collect and pass on.)

USA TODAY Snapshots®

Top workplace frustrations

Poor communication by senior management about the business — 17%

General office politics — 16%

Lack of teamwork — 15%

Having to use politically correct language — 9%

Nosy co-workers — 6%

Source: Opinion Research survey of 1,198 workers. Weighted to actual population proportion.

By Jae Yang and Sam Ward, USA TODAY 2008

If your business sells tangible goods (items you can touch, such as jewelry, clothing, or food), you'll almost certainly have to get a seller's permit. However, even if you sell services, you may need a seller's permit if:

- Your state taxes services (a few states impose a sales tax on services). If you run a service business in one of these states, you may need a permit to collect tax from your customers.

- You provide both goods and services. For example, if you work as a caterer, you might sell both a product (prepared food) and a service (set-up and clean-up, waiting tables, and so on). In this situation, you may need a seller's permit—and you will have to separate what you charge for goods and for services so you can collect sales tax. If you occasionally provide goods in the course of doing your service work (as a plumber might supply a necessary fitting to repair a leak), you generally won't be required to charge your customers sales tax.

If you're caught doing business without a permit, you could be subject to a number of penalties, such as having to pay the sales tax you should have collected from your customers, along with a fine.

FINDING THE FORMS
You can find information on seller's permit requirements at the website of your state's tax agency. For a list of links to these agencies, go to the IRS website at www.irs.gov, choose "Business," then "Small Business/Self-Employed," then "State Links." Or, choose your state's link at the list of tax agencies provided at the website of the federal Small Business Administration at www.sba.gov/hotlist/statetaxhomepages.html.

Permits and Licenses for Specialized Fields

Depending on the type of business you run, you might have to get any number of other permits from your state and local government. For example, you might need a permit from the fire department to run a day care center, a permit from the health department to sell food, or a permit from your state or local environmental agency to do work that involves hazardous chemicals. Your best resources for finding out whether you'll need to meet these requirements are the state and local agencies that regulate your profession. Give them a call or visit their websites (you can find comprehensive links to state and local websites at www.statelocalgov.net).

Working From Home

A retracting economy has prompted many people to think locally. Starting and running a side business is part of that trend. And you can't get any more local than working from home.

Chances are good that you're already operating your side business out of your home. You are in good company—many powerhouse businesses, like Hewlett-Packard, PowerBar, and Avon, started as home-based side businesses. But big or small, home-based businesses create unique issues, which we'll address in this chapter.

Ten Tips for Maximum Home Office Efficiency

If you're operating a side business at home, here are few simple tips that will help you improve your experience.

Home Office Efficiency Tip #1: Draw Limits for Friends and Family

To friends and family, your home-based side business may look like no work at all—they just see you, at home, looking comfortable in jeans or sweats. They may expect to receive your usual level of attention. You'll have to be firm and explain (or repeat) your policy, which might be, "I can take a short break now, but we'll have to schedule anything longer for this afternoon or evening."

Home Office Efficiency Tip #2: Get the Right Internet Connections

In addition to increasing your business efficiency (ask any high-speed addict), broadband is essential for online sellers or companies that do a lot of website modification. Some DSL providers start at $25 to $30 per month (or less). There are many choices, including DSL, cable, satellite, and wireless. Speeds vary depending on the provider and the plan.

Home Office Efficiency Tip #3: Get Organized

Remember the old saying, "A place for everything, and everything in its place"? In a home-based side business, where space is often at a premium, it applies with a vengeance. Keep items you use regularly within easy reach and store the things you use less frequently. Use file folders, desk dividers, bookshelves, and other storage systems to organize your paperwork and project materials. If you're working in a small spot, use vertical space—put shelves, folder racks, or other organizing tools above your workspace.

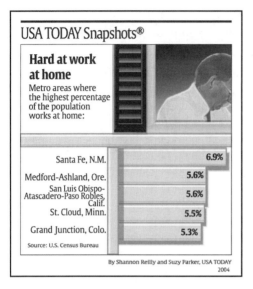

USA TODAY Snapshots®

Hard at work at home

Metro areas where the highest percentage of the population works at home:

Santa Fe, N.M.	6.9%
Medford-Ashland, Ore.	5.6%
San Luis Obispo-Atascadero-Paso Robles, Calif.	5.6%
St. Cloud, Minn.	5.5%
Grand Junction, Colo.	5.3%

Source: U.S. Census Bureau

By Shannon Reilly and Suzy Parker, USA TODAY 2004

Home Office Efficiency Tip #4: Consider Hiring Experts for One-Time Projects

Used sparingly, expert help can really save time and money. If you're facing a one-time task that you don't know how to handle—like designing a website for your side business, remodeling a room to serve as a home office, or developing a company logo—it's much more efficient to pay for a few hours of an expert's time and get the job done right than to try to learn how to do it yourself.

Home Office Efficiency Tip #5: Prioritize

Which activities make money for your side business? Those are the ones you should be spending most of your time on. It seems obvious, but many of us procrastinate or simply fail to prioritize our most important work. When you work at home—where there are so many distractions—business efficiency experts emphasize the importance of getting to the primary business tasks.

Home Office Efficiency Tip #6: Track Your Time

If you're having trouble figuring out where your time is going at home, keep a log of your hours for a couple of weeks, recording what you work on and how long you spend on it. You may be surprised at what you find. For lots of good advice on managing your work time, see *Time Management: Proven Techniques for Making the Most of Your Valuable Time*, by Marshall J. Cook (Adams Media).

Home Office Efficiency Tip #7: Organize Your Phone Connections

It may pay for you to have a separate business line (unless you don't mind it when your teenager ties up your only line). On the other hand, you may be able to sort through personal and business calls on one phone using caller ID (or similar features). You may also want to consider checking VOIP phones (these send phone calls via the Internet) from providers such as Skype.com or Gmail's phone features. These systems save lots of money for businesses that make international calls. Whatever phone system you devise, get a headset. Not only will it save you from a sore neck, but it also makes communication clearer and allows you to keep your hands free to use your computer or search for paperwork.

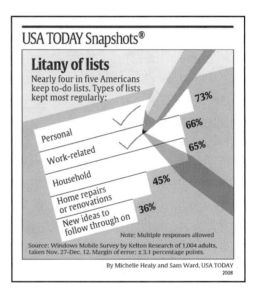

USA TODAY Snapshots®

Litany of lists

Nearly four in five Americans keep to-do lists. Types of lists kept most regularly:

Personal — 73%
Work-related — 66%
Household — 65%
Home repairs or renovations — 45%
New ideas to follow through on — 36%

Note: Multiple responses allowed

Source: Windows Mobile Survey by Kelton Research of 1,004 adults, taken Nov. 27-Dec. 12. Margin of error: ± 3.1 percentage points.

By Michelle Healy and Sam Ward, USA TODAY 2008

Home Office Efficiency Tip #8: Save Money When Buying Home Office Furniture

You don't have to break the bank to outfit your home office. Look at garage sales, used furniture stores or furniture outlets, and websites, such as eBay or Craigslist (www.craigslist.org). You might be able to find a business that has closed and is selling off its equipment on the cheap. For inexpensive new furniture, Office Depot and IKEA are good bets. You can find an extensive list of links to the websites of office furniture companies at www.homefurnish.com; click "Home Office," then "Products."

Home Office Efficiency Tip #9: Spend Some Money on a Decent Chair

If you're spending hours in front of a monitor, a good office chair is a must for ergonomics and comfort. We know we told you to save money on home office furnishings, but we also want you to avoid back and neck problems (which will definitely decrease your side-business efficiency). So be prepared to pay more for a decent office chair. Among the features to look for are adjustable height and tilt, lumbar support, and padded, adjustable armrests. For an article that explains the various features available and what they do, go to www.office-ergo.com and click "Ergonomic Chairs." You can also find plenty of information on office ergonomics at the website of the UCLA Ergonomics Program, at http://ergonomics.ucla.edu.

USA TODAY Snapshots®

Generation X is all about flexibility

Younger workers are more interested in having flexible working hours:

Generation X **76%**

Baby boomers **67%**

Seniors **57%**

Note: Generation X ages 26 to 40, baby boomers ages 41 to 59 and seniors ages 60 and over.

Source: Randstad North America survey of 3,233 respondents ages 18 and older. Margin of error ±2 percentage points.

By Jae Yang and Bob Laird, USA TODAY 2005

Home Office Efficiency Tip #10: Get the Right Work Surface

For your desk or work surface, you'll want something that gives you enough space to work and sits at the right height. Using a work surface that's too small is inefficient—it means you'll have to scatter your equipment and other materials around the room instead of having them all within easy reach.

Home Office Efficiency Tip #11: Watch Your Weight

When we asked home-based side-business owners about the pitfalls of working at home, many of them mentioned weight gain. It's one of the hazards of sharing a workplace with your refrigerator. Those long late-night hours that it often takes to get a new side business off the ground can also take a toll. Healthy eating habits and regular exercise routines fall by the wayside when we spend all of our time trying to maintain two jobs. You already know the health risks associated with weight gain, so keep that in mind the next time you're at the computer and you reach for that bag of Oreos.

The "Sweet" Sounds of Your Circular Saw

One of the most common triggers for neighbor complaints is noise. So if you need to run that drill press at 5 a.m., keep in mind that will likely result in zoning investigations and may violate local municipal noise ordinances. Before operating noisy machinery, check your local noise ordinance at your library or check out the Noise Pollution Clearinghouse (www.nonoise.org).

Self-Assessment: When Should You Move Your Side Business Out of Your Home?

You already know the benefits of working at home: low cost, flexibility, and no commute. Sure, there are also distractions, but before you consider moving your side business to a leased space, rented studio, or nearby office complex, consider the following questions.

How Much Are You Saving?

Start by looking at the economics of your home business. You won't have to pay any additional rent or mortgage to run your business from home. Compare that to the price of commercial real estate in your area—at a minimum, you would be paying $10 per square foot per month for commercial space. Other costs—equipment, insurance, and services—may be roughly the same whether you work at home or in an outside space. And either way, your business costs are tax deductible. If you will have to build additional space or do extensive remodeling to create a place to work at home, you'll have to figure that extra cost into your calculations.

Do You Have the Right Space?

Sure it's free, but does your home give you enough space—and the right kind of space—for your side business? Do you need to provide a sitting area for clients or customers? If you are selling or making products, do you have space to store your inventory and supplies? If your side business requires a lot of equipment, do you have the room to set it up so you can use it efficiently? When you consider space, think about the future, too. Do you anticipate ever having employees? If so, the conventional wisdom is that you'll need at least 150 to 200 square feet per employee. If your business is growing quickly, maybe it's time to consider the home office as a transitional space and start looking beyond your property boundaries.

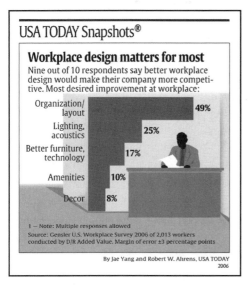

USA TODAY Snapshots®

Workplace design matters for most

Nine out of 10 respondents say better workplace design would make their company more competitive. Most desired improvement at workplace:

Organization/layout — 49%
Lighting, acoustics — 25%
Better furniture, technology — 17%
Amenities — 10%
Decor — 8%

1 — Note: Multiple responses allowed
Source: Gensler U.S. Workplace Survey 2006 of 2,013 workers conducted by D/R Added Value. Margin of error ±3 percentage points

By Jae Yang and Robert W. Ahrens, USA TODAY 2006

Does Your Home Send the Right Message for Your Side Business?

If clients or customers will come to your business, you'll have to consider whether you can make your home business space look professional enough to inspire confidence in visitors. It can be tough to look like an entrepreneur when the entrance to your office is cluttered with children's toys, your desk doubles as your dining room table, or your workspace resides in a spare closet. Can you modify your home to create a businesslike atmosphere? Do you have a separate entrance or a structure (such as a converted garage) that clients can get to without traversing a lot of living areas? Is your work area safe? Do you have aggressive dogs, tripping hazards, or low-hanging beams?

Will You Have to Contend with Zoning, Lease, or Homeowners' Association Restrictions?

Depending on where you live, zoning laws, lease restrictions, or subdivision rules (covenants, conditions, and restrictions, or CC&Rs) may affect your ability to run your side business from your home. For example, zoning laws may limit or prohibit signs or visible advertising on a residence. These rules may prohibit employees other than domestic help, limit noise levels (typically through imposing "quiet hours" in the evening and early morning), or prohibit any enterprise that would increase traffic or competition for scarce parking spaces. If such a prohibition applies, you might be able to get around it by applying for a variance (an exception to a zoning law), figuring out a way to provide more parking, or limiting your work hours, for example.

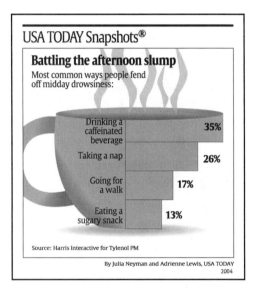

USA TODAY Snapshots®

Battling the afternoon slump

Most common ways people fend off midday drowsiness:

Drinking a caffeinated beverage — 35%

Taking a nap — 26%

Going for a walk — 17%

Eating a sugary snack — 13%

Source: Harris Interactive for Tylenol PM

By Julia Neyman and Adrienne Lewis, USA TODAY 2004

Will Your Home Business Disturb the Neighbors?

As a practical matter, the only way you are likely to get caught for violating zoning or other restrictions is if your neighbors turn you in to local authorities. And unless you have particularly mean-spirited neighbors, they are likely to report you to authorities only if your business causes problems for them—for example, if you make noise late at night, your employees park in front of their driveways, or the comings and goings of your clients lead neighbors to think you might be up to something shady.

Can People Reach You?

If clients, customers, employees, or others will visit you at home, they'll need to be able to get there—which is easier if you live close to public transit or are otherwise easy to reach. The same is true of vendors and service providers, such as those for mail and package delivery. Some companies (notably UPS) charge more to make deliveries to a home office than to a commercial address. This may not be a home office deal breaker, but you should factor any additional charges into your calculations.

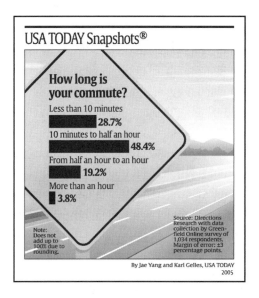

USA TODAY Snapshots®

How long is your commute?

Less than 10 minutes
28.7%
10 minutes to half an hour
48.4%
From half an hour to an hour
19.2%
More than an hour
3.8%

Note: Does not add up to 100% due to rounding.

Source: Directions Research with data collection by Green-field Online survey of 1,034 respondents. Margin of error: ±3 percentage points.

By Jae Yang and Karl Gelles, USA TODAY 2005

Is There Sufficient Parking?

If customers, suppliers, or others will come to your home business, they'll need to be able to park. Do you have space on your property for their cars? If not, does your neighborhood have any restrictions that will make parking difficult, such as a required sticker or permit? If you live in a housing development, visitors' parking may be restricted. And in densely populated cities, it may be tough to find parking under any circumstances. If you can rent a garage or parking spaces from neighbors or create a parking area on your property, you might solve the problem. But don't ask customers or clients to park in your driveway if doing so would block the sidewalk—this will get your customers a hefty ticket in many urban areas and may also provoke the wrath of pedestrians, especially those with disabilities or baby strollers.

Can You Get the Insurance You Need?

Every business—even a small one run from home—should be insured against common hazards and events. Even if you already have home-owner's or renter's insurance, most policies either don't cover home businesses at all, or provide only about $2,500 worth of protection for losses to business property. Because just one uninsured loss could easily put you out of business, you absolutely must protect yourself. If your existing policy doesn't offer enough (or any) protection, you can probably get some basic protection from a home business rider. Talk to your insurance agent.

Never Answer Mommy's Phone

Many parents start side businesses so they can spend more time with their children at home. But it can be a true challenge to carve out uninterrupted time to work—and to maintain a business image. Side-business parents often come up with a combination of rules for their older children (including a ban on touching the business phone) and flexibility to accommodate the needs of younger ones.

You can find a lot of great information for work-at-home parents on the Web—simply type "home business" and "parents," "mothers," or "fathers" into your favorite search engine to find dozens of sites. A good place to start is The Parent's Home Office, at www.parentshomeoffice.com; it has lots of helpful articles on childproofing your home office, activities to keep kids busy while you work, and much more.

How Much Security Do You Need?

Are you prepared to open your living space to customers or service providers you don't know well? Or does your business need the kinds of safety measures afforded by many commercial workplaces, such as security guards, identification badges or other means of limiting access to the facility, and alarm systems? If you have a lot of valuable business equipment and tools, can you safeguard them adequately in your home or driveway?

Studios and Storage: When You Need More Space

If you're making or selling goods, you may need additional studio or storage space for your home business, either to create your goods or manage your inventory. Assuming you don't need a retail space, your best bet is usually to find convenient, low-cost, utilitarian surroundings, preferably among other similar small businesses. Here are some issues to keep in mind when you're thinking of leasing commercial space.

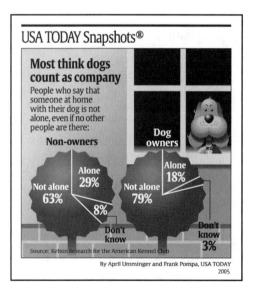

USA TODAY Snapshots®

Most think dogs count as company

People who say that someone at home with their dog is not alone, even if no other people are there:

Non-owners
Alone 29%
Not alone 63%
8%
Don't know

Dog owners
Alone 18%
Not alone 79%
Don't know 3%

Source: Kelton Research for the American Kennel Club

By April Umminger and Frank Pompa, USA TODAY
2005

Figure out the total "nut." If you lease studio space, figure out the maximum rent your business can afford to pay per month, determine what type of security deposit you can pay, and consider how much money you can afford to spend to alter the space to fit your studio needs.

Calculating rent gets complicated. Many landlords charge you not only for square footage, but also for other regular expenses, such real estate taxes, utilities, and insurance. If you rent in a multi-tenant building, you're likely to be asked to pay your share of common area maintenance, too. If you rent the entire building, you may be asked to foot the entire bill for these costs.

Security deposits aren't the only up-front costs. Unless you are fortunate enough to find space that was previously owned by a person in the same field as yourself, you'll need to modify the space to fit your needs and tastes. These modifications are known as improvements. You might find a landlord willing to foot the entire bill. But for now, don't count on it. The tenant usually pays for this work. You'll need to determine what it would cost to make your space usable.

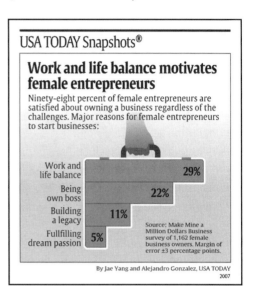

USA TODAY Snapshots®

Work and life balance motivates female entrepreneurs

Ninety-eight percent of female entrepreneurs are satisfied about owning a business regardless of the challenges. Major reasons for female entrepreneurs to start businesses:

- Work and life balance — 29%
- Being own boss — 22%
- Building a legacy — 11%
- Fullfilling dream passion — 5%

Source: Make Mine a Million Dollars Business survey of 1,162 female business owners. Margin of error ±3 percentage points.

By Jae Yang and Alejandro Gonzalez, USA TODAY 2007

How long do you need? If you want the most flexibility, look for space that's offered on a month-to-month basis (month-to-month leases are also called rental agreements). A month-to-month rental automatically renews each month unless you or your landlord gives the other the proper amount of written notice to terminate the agreement. Under a month-to-month agreement, the landlord can raise the rent or change other terms with proper written notice. A long-term lease locks in a good deal for a longer period of time and often saves money on improvements and related transaction costs.

Amenities, security, and comfort. Check your lease for any amenities, such as windows that open; the condition of the heating, ventilating, and air-conditioning system (HVAC); whether there's soundproofing; who controls the thermostat; whether there's any storage space, parking, security, and the ability to expand your space.

Is subleasing for you? You may be able to get a great deal as a subtenant. As long as the tenant's own lease allows it, subleasing is one way to cut the overhead. There are, however, downsides to being a subtenant. For one, you're dealing with someone who is not in the business of being a landlord and may not know or care about treating a tenant—that is, you—properly and legally. Check to see for yourself whether the landlord's consent is needed for subletting the space or assigning the lease. If it is, don't finalize your agreement with the tenant until the landlord has consented in writing. Also, get written confirmation from the landlord and tenant that the tenant's lease is in good standing, and that as long as you pay your rent and other required charges, you can continue to occupy your space. ●

Working With Others

W e're aware that the vast majority of side-business owners do not (and will not) hire employees (90% of home businesses don't have them). But side-business owners often hire independent contractors, and, equally important, side business owners—particularly those who provide services—are often in the position of being independent contractors. In this chapter, we'll discuss some independent contractor issues and we'll also discuss a special kind of side-business worker—your spouse or children—and how their participation affects your side business.

Employee vs. Independent Contractor: What's the Difference?

An independent contractor (IC) is usually a person who provides specialized services on a per-project basis for a number of businesses. Some common examples of ICs include plumbers, architects, bookkeepers, and piano tuners. An IC is hired to provide a service, usually one that requires a certain level of skill, experience, and sometimes licensing. ICs can be hired on an ongoing basis—for example, to maintain a website, or handle accounting. ICs also work by the job—for example, to remodel a home office or help a business launch a product line.

USA TODAY Snapshots®

Is it important for managers to have a sense of humor?

Yes
97%

No
3%

Source: Robert Half International survey of 492 workers. Margin of error ±4 percentage points.

By Jae Yang and Marcy E. Mullins, USA TODAY
2007

An employee, on the other hand, is not running his or her own business. An employee follows the rules and obeys the standards required by the employer. An employer exercises a lot more control over an employee than over an IC, from setting work hours to imposing a dress code to dictating exactly how the employee does every aspect of the job. Although employees can be hired for a short-term project (such as helping you with a seasonal mailing crunch or gift-wrapping items during a holiday rush), it's more common to hire employees on an open-ended basis, until the work runs out or the employee quits or doesn't meet your expectations.

USA TODAY Snapshots®

Job candidate mistakes
In which job-application areas do candidates make the most mistakes?

Interview 32%

Résumé 21%

9% Cover letter

9% Reference checks

7% Interview follow-up

6% Screening call

2% Other

14% Don't know

Source: Robert Half Finance & Accounting survey of 1,414 CFOs of U.S. companies with 20 or more employees. Margin of error ±2 percentage points.

By Jae Yang and Sam Ward, USA TODAY 2006

When businesses misclassify a worker, they often run into problems with the state unemployment insurance agency, the state workers' compensation board, and the IRS. (The IRS, in particular, imposes hefty penalties for misclassification.) The IRS test considers workers employees if the company they work for has the right to direct and control the way they work—including the details of when, where, and how the job is accomplished. In contrast, the IRS considers workers independent contractors if the company they work for does not manage how they work, except to accept or reject their final results.

The important thing to remember here is not to treat workers as ICs if they are really employees. If you're attempting to avoid taxes and legal requirements—for example you're treating someone as an IC so you won't have to worry about overtime, rest breaks, antidiscrimination rules, providing time off, or dealing with payroll deductions—there are a number of government agencies that might call your bluff (no government agency is ever going to tell you that you should have classified an employee as an independent contractor). If you're curious about how the IRS makes its consideration, here are some factors that it uses.

Factors the IRS Considers	
Factors That Make a Worker Look Like an IC	**Factors That Make a Worker Look Like an Employee**
Worker can earn a profit or suffer a loss from the activity.	Worker is paid for his or her time, regardless of how well or poorly the hiring company is doing.
Worker furnishes the tools and materials needed to do the work.	Worker receives tools and materials from the hiring business.
Worker is paid by the job.	Worker is paid by the hour.
Worker decides how to do the work.	Worker receives instructions and training on how to do the work.
Worker decides when and where to work.	Worker has set hours, usually at the hiring company's place of business.
Worker hires and pays any assistants.	Worker's assistants (if any) are provided and paid for by the hiring company.
Worker pays for business and travel expenses.	Worker's job-related expenses are paid by the hiring company.
Worker works for more than one business at a time.	Worker provides services to only one business.
Worker does not receive employee benefits from hiring company.	Worker receives employee benefits from hiring company.
Worker can be terminated only for reasons specified in contract.	Worker can quit or be fired at any time.
Worker provides services that fall outside of the hiring company's usual operations.	Worker provides services that are an integral part of the hiring company's regular operations.

Five Reasons Why Hiring an IC Is Usually a Better Choice For Your Side Business

If you're considering hiring someone for your side business, you're usually going to want to hire an IC. Here's why.

Reason #1: ICs Require Less Training

Unlike an employee, whom you may have to train, an IC will be ready to go on Day One and will have the skill and background to do the job right. ICs also have a stronger incentive to finish the work quickly.

Reason #2: ICs Are Always a Better Choice for Short-Term Tasks

If you have a specific project or task you need done (for example, a one-time electrical job or help designing your packaging), you'll probably want to go with an IC.

Reason #3: Costs Are Lower With ICs

Your total cash outlay will probably be lower for ICs than employees. Although an IC is likely to charge you more to do a project than you'd have to actually pay an employee, employees are more expensive overall after you add on taxes, insurance costs, the price of equipment, materials, and workspace, and other cash outlays.

Reason #4: ICs Are Better for Your Cash Flow

State and federal laws set strict guidelines for paying employees. You have to pay at least the minimum hourly wage, and you have to pay them according to a schedule set by state law (anywhere from once a week to once a month). If you don't follow these rules, you could face fines and penalties. For an IC, you and the IC will set the pay schedule yourselves. If your clients pay you by the project, you can pay the IC when you get paid. If you won't be able to pay for a while, you can work out an installment arrangement with the IC.

Reason #5: ICs Require Fewer Rules and Red Tape

Unless you're ready to learn your legal obligations as an employer and set up a payroll system to withhold taxes and pay them over to the IRS, don't hire employees. You can run into trouble quickly if you don't handle employee matters by the book; for an IC, on the other hand, the paperwork is minimal. Keep in mind, however, that government agencies will take a close look at ICs to make sure they shouldn't have been classified as employees. This means you may be a more likely target for an audit if you hire ICs.

Don't hire an IC to do anything other than a very minor project without signing

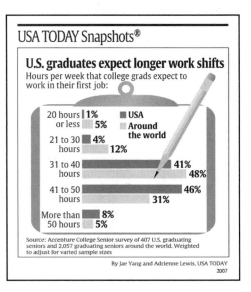

USA TODAY Snapshots®

U.S. graduates expect longer work shifts
Hours per week that college grads expect to work in their first job:

	USA	Around the world
20 hours or less	1%	5%
21 to 30 hours	4%	12%
31 to 40 hours	41%	48%
41 to 50 hours	46%	31%
More than 50 hours	8%	5%

Source: Accenture College Senior survey of 407 U.S. graduating seniors and 2,057 graduating seniors around the world. Weighted to adjust for varied sample sizes

By Jae Yang and Adrienne Lewis, USA TODAY 2007

an agreement. An IC agreement helps you and the IC clarify the terms of your deal, creates a written record of exactly what you agreed upon, and can help convince the IRS and other agencies that you and the IC did not intend to create an employer–employee relationship. A written agreement is especially important if you are hiring someone to do creative work for you—artwork, inventing, or design, for example. An IC will own the creative rights to the work unless you make a written agreement signing the rights over to you. For help creating a written IC agreement, take a look at *Consultant & Independent Contractor Agreements*, by Stephen Fishman (Nolo).

Legal and Paperwork Requirements: ICs

There are only a couple of legal rules you have to follow when hiring an IC—and they kick in only when the hiring party pays the IC $600 or more in one year.

Complete and File IRS Form 1099-MISC, *Miscellaneous Income*

This form is very straightforward—you simply enter identifying information about your business and the IC, then enter the amount you paid the IC in the box marked "Nonemployee compensation." You must provide copies of the form to the IC no later than January 31 of the year after you made the payment. You also have to file copies of the form with the IRS and your state taxing authority (you have to file with the IRS by February 28 of the year after you made the payment; check with your state tax agency to learn its filing deadline). When you file the 1099 with the IRS, you must send along IRS Form 1096, *Annual Summary and Transmission of U.S. Information Returns.* Form 1096 is essentially a cover letter on which you add up all payments you reported on 1099 forms for the year.

USA TODAY Snapshots®

Employees want to make a difference

What do you think is the most important factor in job success? Top factors:

Using my talents to make a difference — 36%
Financial success — 29%
New opportunities — 13%
Creating new solutions to existing problems — 9%
Being able to give back to my community and society at large — 9%

Source: Ace Hardware survey of 1,059 adults 18 and older conducted by Impulse Research. Margin of error ±3 percentage points.

By Jae Yang and Adrienne Lewis, USA TODAY 2008

FINDING THE FORMS
Although you can download both Form 1099 and Form 1096 from the IRS website, www.irs.gov, you cannot file these copies electronically. Instead, you must file an original of each, which you can get by contacting your local IRS office (you can find a list of offices at the IRS website) or calling 800-TAX-FORM.

Get the IC's Taxpayer Identification Number

The IRS knows that many ICs work under the table—they're paid in cash, which they don't report (or they underreport) to the IRS. To put a stop to this, the IRS requires those who hire ICs to get a copy of their taxpayer ID, which is their employer identification number or Social Security number, which they use on their tax returns. If an IC won't give you an ID number or the IRS informs you that the number the IC gave you is incorrect, you have to withhold taxes from the IC's pay and remit that money to the IRS. (The IRS calls this backup withholding.) Obviously, you want to avoid this extra chore—and you can, by requiring the IC to fill out IRS Form W-9, *Request for Taxpayer Identification Number*. If the IC doesn't have an ID number yet, you don't have to start withholding until 60 days after he or she applies for one.

Legal and Paperwork Requirements: Employees

There are more forms to fill in—and rules to follow—when you hire an employee than when you hire an IC. Fortunately, most of the paperwork is fairly simple, and you can find the forms online. When you hire an employee, you must do all of the following.

Have the Employee Complete IRS Form W-4, *Employee's Withholding Allowance Certificate*

On this form, the employee provides basic identifying information and tells you how much money to withhold from each paycheck. You must have this form in your files, but you don't have to send it to the IRS.

> **FINDING THE FORMS**
> You can download W-4 forms from the IRS website, www.irs.gov, or get them by contacting your local IRS office (you can find a list of offices at the IRS website) or calling 800-TAX-FORM.

Complete USCIS Form I-9, *Employment Eligibility Verification*

This form confirms that the employee is eligible to work in the United States. The employee must complete a portion of the form and then give you documentation of his or her eligibility. The form tells you what kinds of documents are acceptable. A U.S. passport or a driver's license and birth certificate or Social Security card are the typical showing for U.S. citizens. You don't have to file this form, but you must keep it on hand for three years after you hire the employee or one year after the employee quits or is fired, whichever is later.

FINDING THE FORMS
You can download I-9 forms from the website of the United States Citizenship and Immigration Services (USCIS, formerly the INS), at www.uscis.gov. You can fill in the form on your computer or print out a blank copy and fill it in by hand. I-9s can now be completed and stored entirely electronically, signatures and all; check the USCIS website for more information.

Report the Employee to Your State's New-Hire Reporting Agency

Employers must give basic information on new employees to the state, which uses that information to track down parents who owe child support. You will have to submit your employee's name, address, and Social Security number; some states require additional information, such as the employee's date of birth or first day of work.

FINDING THE FORMS
To get the information and forms you need, start at the website of the Administration for Children and Families, a subdivision of the federal Department of Health and Human Services. Click the tab for "Working with ACF," then scroll down to the heading "Employer Info." This will lead you to several publications about the new-hire reporting program, as well as a list of state requirements and links to the agency in each state that administers the program. Go to your state agency's website to download the required form and find out what information you have to provide.

Get an Employer Identification Number (EIN) From the IRS

An employer identification number (EIN) is a nine-digit number, like an individual's Social Security number, that's used by the federal government to identify your business for tax purposes. Your business must have an EIN if you have at least one employee. We explain how to obtain an EIN in Chapter 6.

Register With Your State's Labor Department

Once you hire an employee, you will have to pay state unemployment taxes. These payments go to your state's unemployment compensation fund, which provides short-term relief to workers who lose their jobs. Typically, you must complete some initial registration paperwork, then pay money into the fund periodically. Unemployment compensation is a form of insurance, so the amount you pay will depend, in part, on how many of your former employees file for unemployment (just as your insurance premiums depend, in part, on how many claims you file against the policy).

FINDING THE FORMS

Start at the federal Department of Labor, which administers federal/state unemployment programs. Go to http://workforcesecurity .doleta.gov/map.asp, which provides a link to each state's unemployment agency. Once you get to your state agency's website, look for a tab or link on unemployment, or find the material for employers or businesses. Many states provide downloadable forms and online information on your responsibilities.

Workers' Compensation Insurance

Many states require all employers to have workers' comp coverage, either by paying into a state fund or buying a separate policy. Some states exempt employers with no more than two or three employees from this rule, but it might make sense to purchase coverage anyway. Beyond the legal requirements, having workers' comp coverage can save you a bundle if one of your employees is hurt on the job.

Hang Up Required Posters

Even the smallest businesses are legally required to post certain notices to let employees know their rights under a variety of workplace laws. The federal government wants you to put up a handful of notices; many states have additional posting requirements.

 FINDING THE FORMS
The Department of Labor's website, www.dol.gov, lists workplace posters. (Search for "posters" in the A–Z index to find what you need.) Your state's labor department probably also has any required posters on its website. If you're having trouble figuring out which requirements apply to you (or you don't want to post a dozen different notices), you can get an all-in-one poster that combines all required state and federal notices from your local chamber of commerce for about $20.

Ten Tips When Hiring Family Members

As Tony Soprano can attest, there's something to be gained by bringing the family into the business—for example, loyalty, respect, and a sense of mission. Besides that, family businesses have a better chance of survival over the first five years than nonfamily businesses (they also make up a third of companies on the S&P 500 and contribute more than half of the national payroll). But working with family members can also trigger emotional, legal, and business issues. Here are ten things you should know about making your side business a family business.

Family Business Tip #1: Family Members Are Easy to Hire and Hard to Fire

How do you know whether to bring a family member into your business? First consider whether they share your vision or interest in the business. Next, consider whether they're competent. Neil Koenig, author of *You Can't Fire Me, I'm Your Father* (Hillsboro Press), suggests a simple standard. Just ask: "Is this person hirable at our competitors?" If not, don't consider the relative for a job. If you're unsure about qualifications, business counselor James Hutcheson suggests asking family members to come in for a short specified period of time to avoid painful terminations if things don't pan out.

Family Business Tip #2: Family Businesses Affect the Family's Bottom Line

Don't bring in a spouse (or other relative) until you project the short- and long-term impact on your family balance sheet, especially if the spouse must curtail other money-making (or money-saving) activities.

Family Business Tip #3: Be Clear With Directions and Compensation

You should be able to explain to your spouse or child how long and how often their help will be needed—for example, weekly, monthly, or seasonally. Accurately describe the work and spell out the type and variety of tasks. Says business author Jill Lublin, "In the case of spouses working together, it's crucial that the division of duties is clear. Each spouse should do their job and then get the heck out of the other one's way."

Compensation must be reasonable. If not, you'll likely trigger resentment or disputes that will soon spill over to the dinner table.

USA TODAY Snapshots®

All in the family
Do you plan to bring your children into the family business?

No **43%**
Undecided **31%**
Yes **26%**

Source: SunTrust Bank Private Wealth Management survey of 201 business owners of companies with revenue of $10 million or more.

By Jae Yang and and Bob Laird, USA TODAY 2007

Family Business Tip #4: Establish Boundaries for Family Members

For most people, the boundary between work and family is clear, but that's not always the case when a family member joins the business.

"If you can't turn it off at home," says business counselor Dr. Rachna Jain, "your whole relationship rises and falls with the business." One approach is to establish no-biztalk zones or ban business discussions during certain times (such as dinner).

Family Business Tip #5: Take Advantage of Tax Benefits When Hiring Kids

If you hire your children, you can deduct the salaries you pay them. Your children, particularly those under age 18, probably pay taxes on this income at a lower tax rate (starting at 10% for amounts under $8,025) than you pay on your business income. Not only that, a minor child who performs services for the family business does not have to pay any taxes on the first $5,450 in wages earned in a year (as of 2008). If your child is under 18, you don't even need to pay payroll taxes—that is, payments such as FICA (Social Security and Medicare) and FUTA (federal unemployment) that are required for all other employees. Even more tax can be saved if the child establishes an IRA, the contributions for which are tax deductible up to $5,000 per year. In that case, your working offspring won't have to pay taxes on the first $10,450 of earned income. For more information on employing your child, see IRS Publication 929, *Tax Rules for Children and Dependents*.

USA TODAY Snapshots®

What employees want
What aspect is important when your employer communicates with you? Top responses:

Giving insights on how to be more effective **52%**
Showing how to fit into the company's vision **47%**
Explaining the company's vision **45%**
Engaging on a personal level **41%**

Note: Multiple responses allowed
Source: Jack Morton Worldwide Experiential Marketing Global Consumer Response survey of 1,625 workers and job seekers conducted by Sponsorship Research International. Margin of error ±2 percentage points.
By Jae Yang and Marcy E. Mullins, USA TODAY 2006

Keep in mind that these rules don't apply for hiring anyone's kids—only your own. If the IRS questions you, the primary concern will be whether the child does real work and is paid reasonable wages. In general, as long as you are paying for a task you would pay someone else to do—for example, sweeping up the studio, putting stamps on promotional postcards, running errands, doing clerical tasks, entering data into a computer, or answering the phones—and as long as the payment is commensurate with what you might pay an outsider, the IRS will likely accept the categorization.

Family Business Tip #6: Hire Your Parents

If you hire your retired parents, you can deduct the expense, lowering your taxable income. Your parents will probably be taxed at a lower tax rate than what you pay. But before Mom and Dad punch the time clock, check what effect the extra income will have on their Social Security. In some cases—for example, for parents under 65, income from your business could reduce their Social Security income.

Family Business Tip #7: Understand Spousal Co-Ownership Rules

If spouses own a business in a community property state (Arizona, California, Idaho, Nevada, New Mexico, Texas, Washington, or Wisconsin), they can report their business income on a Schedule C (as a sole proprietorship) as part of the joint return. This doesn't save money but it does save the time and hassle of filing a K-1 partnership return, which is required of spouses who co-own a business in a non-community property state. If one spouse owns the business and the other works for it, however, it's a sole proprietorship, and income is reported on the individual family member's tax return.

Family Business Tip #8: Tread Carefully With Family Limited Partnerships

Family limited partnerships (FLPs) are a business form popularized in the 1990s that shields a business from many liabilities and provides tax benefits, especially when you're transferring assets of the business to another generation. In the typical FLP, the parents act as the general partners. The children are the passive limited partners, who cannot run the business and are prevented from transferring their interest to others outside of the family. If the parents are sued, the business assets of the limited partners can't be touched by creditors.

Using FLPs, savvy accountants and lawyers have helped family businesses achieve nearly tax-free transfers of millions of dollars of money and business property to their heirs. Chances are that you won't need to think about FLPs for your family business because the tax benefits usually won't kick in unless your family has millions in assets. In any case, the IRS is suspicious of FLPs. In 2004, a federal tax court knocked out a Texas FLP, obligating heirs to pay over $2 million in taxes. In another 2004 case, however, a court of appeal upheld an FLP, though it stated that a transaction

USA TODAY Snapshots®

Employers confident of workers' skill

How would you rate the overall skill level of your organization's workforce?

Better than competitors **43%**

About equal to competitors **39%**

Industry-leading **14%**

Non-existent **1%**

Worse than competitors **3%**

Source: Accenture The High-Performance Workforce study of 251 executives.

By Jae Yang and Keith Simmons, USA TODAY 2006

between family members will be scrutinized more thoroughly to assure that the arrangement is not a sham transaction or a disguised gift. (*Kimbell v. U.S.*, 371 F.3d 257 (5th Cir. 2004).) In short, tread carefully and with the sound advice of an attorney or accountant before forming an FLP.

Family Business Tip #9: Beware of Divorce Business Style

After divorce, even if only one spouse operated the business, the ownership will likely be split between both. Unless there is an agreement to the contrary—for example, a prenuptial or buyout agreement—divorce laws generally require that the value of the business ownership be split by the separating spouses. In community property states (Arizona, California, Idaho, Louisiana, Nevada, New Mexico, Texas, Washington, and Wisconsin), each spouse is entitled to an equal share unless the business was acquired with one spouse's separate property. In other states, a similar rule makes each spouse entitled to an equitable (fair) share of the business.

Most ownership issues can be anticipated with a buyout agreement (also known as a buy-sell agreement). Buyout agreements are like a prenuptial agreement for your business. They can require that a person sell an ownership interest back to the company or to other co-owners, according to a valuation method provided in the agreement. Preparing the valuation can be tricky, which is why a buyout agreement can be helpful. It establishes a way to put a value on the business and usually requires that the value of the business be calculated on two dates: marriage and divorce. An attorney can assist in preparing a buyout agreement or you can prepare one yourself by reading *Business Buyout Agreements: A Step-by-Step Guide for Co-Owners*, by Bethany Laurence and Anthony Mancuso (Nolo).

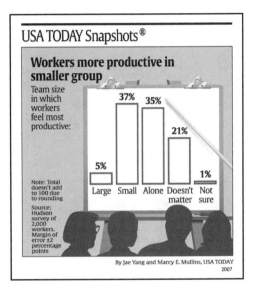

USA TODAY Snapshots®

Workers more productive in smaller group

Team size in which workers feel most productive:

Large 5%
Small 37%
Alone 35%
Doesn't matter 21%
Not sure 1%

Note: Total doesn't add to 100 due to rounding

Source: Hudson survey of 2,000 workers. Margin of error ±2 percentage points

By Jae Yang and Marcy E. Mullins, USA TODAY 2007

Family Business Tip #10: Incorporating the Family Business May Save Money at Tax Time

Incorporation has extra benefits when family members work in the business. If you incorporate the family business, you can shift income from higher tax brackets to lower ones (known as income splitting) by giving stock to family members in lower tax brackets—for example, giving stock to kids younger than 14. ●

Marketing Basics

I f you ask five customers how they learned about your business and they tell you it was from satisfied customers, you can probably skip this chapter. There is no better, more cost-effective form of marketing than word-of-mouth. If new business comes by referral, then you already have a marketing team in action: your customers.

If you aren't getting new customers or keeping the ones you have, you may need a marketing fix. We'll provide some help in this chapter. As you read, keep a few things in mind.

Sophisticated marketing help is readily available. Cartons of books and hundreds of websites can advise you how to redo your packaging, get publicity, write newspaper ads, buy radio advertising, design new brochures, make television ads, or update your website with more pizzazz (though we're not really sure websites need more pizzazz). We recommend many of these resources throughout this chapter.

There are no one-size-fits-all rules when it comes to marketing. You may be able to handle all of your marketing with a well-designed booth at a national trade show or with a series of beautifully designed postcards. What works for you depends on your personality and your business. For example, a gregarious, extroverted business owner may be well-suited for live product demonstrations and similar public events. But an arty, introverted business owner may do a better job of reaching customers with personalized letters or customized mailings. Our advice is to explore the marketing resources available and choose what feels right for you and your business.

Think about marketing in a very broad way. It goes far beyond the tools discussed in this chapter. Everything you do in your daily business activity becomes part of your marketing effort: The way you greet customers, ship orders, handle refunds, or maintain your work space can have a greater influence on business success than your choice of business cards or the purchase of radio spots. Many business owners have learned the hard way that the most successful marketing is working hard to maintain the integrity and credibility at the heart of your business.

What's the Difference? Marketing vs. Advertising

Marketing is any method of attracting and retaining customers. Marketing includes advertising. Advertising is when you pay to spread your message via the Internet, TV, radio, a newspaper or magazine, or any other medium. So, if you paint the name of your business on the side of your truck, that's marketing; if you pay someone to paint the name of your business on their truck, it's advertising. Think of advertising as one of many marketing tools. Why make the distinction? As you'll see, some marketing experts believe that advertising is the wrong route for small business owners.

Ten Marketing Tips

You want to formulate a marketing strategy that reflects your personality and your business. To help you achieve that goal, here are some ideas and suggestions.

Marketing Tip #1: You Can Avoid Advertising

If you buy only one marketing book, we recommend *Marketing Without Advertising*, by Michael Phillips and Salli Rasberry (Nolo), a book that changed the way many small business owners thought about marketing. Considering that the average consumer is exposed to 60% more daily advertising today than 15 years ago, it's no wonder that Phillips and Rasberry want you to avoid paying for ad space. They point out that more than two-thirds of the profitable small businesses in the United States operate without advertising and urge you to concentrate on creating a high-quality operation that customers, employees, and other businesspeople will trust, respect, and recommend. Their key strategies are built around getting customers to spread the word, planning marketing events that keep customers involved, and encouraging the media to comment positively on your business. We'll discuss some of these strategies in more detail, below.

Marketing Tip #2: Drive Customers by Need, Price, and Access

As part of your marketing strategy, consider the common factors that drive customers to a business. In *How to Run a Thriving Business* (Nolo), Ralph Warner advises that there are three elements of success:

- **Need.** When considering how to market or which tools to use, think about why customers need your products or services instead of those of your competitors. For example, customers seeking computer repair may need house calls or evening maintenance— two qualities that could distinguish your marketing strategy.

- **Price.** Some customers base purchasing decisions primarily on price; others go for value. Figure out your typical customers and price accordingly. In either case, people like prices that are clear,

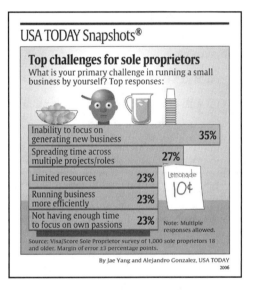

USA TODAY Snapshots®

Top challenges for sole proprietors
What is your primary challenge in running a small business by yourself? Top responses:

Inability to focus on generating new business	35%
Spreading time across multiple projects/roles	27%
Limited resources	23%
Running business more efficiently	23%
Not having enough time to focus on own passions	23%

Note: Multiple responses allowed.

Source: Visa/Score Sole Proprietor survey of 1,000 sole proprietors 18 and older. Margin of error ±3 percentage points.

By Jae Yang and Alejandro Gonzalez, USA TODAY 2006

easy to understand, and not hidden. No one likes pricing surprises. And, if possible, give consumers some control over pricing. Retailers such as Costco and Amazon.com are built on this principle—offering consumers the ability to save money by choosing among pricing options.

- **Access.** If cost and quality are equal, customers usually patronize the business that's easiest to access. What matters is whether customers can find your business and patronize it once they locate it. To help them, you need good signage, parking, and clear yellow pages listings. Access can also translate into your Web business. How easy is it for customers to find you on the Web? And equally important, does your website describe how to contact or locate your business?

Marketing Tip #3: Market After the Sale

Some of your best marketing can happen after a sale is made. For example, after customers buy Gunnar Madsen's compact disc of waltz music at CDBaby.com, they receive an email offering free downloads of Gunnar's other music. Later, he writes to customers offering to place them on his mailing list. Author Seth Godin calls this "permission marketing," and he has written a book of the same name. The basic principle: Once the customer responds to your offer, you can get permission to sell more stuff. In other words, the sale is the beginning of the relationship, not the end.

Marketing Tip #4: Go Guerrilla

Check out Jay Levinson's *Guerrilla Marketing* (Houghton Mifflin), the first marketing book aimed squarely at small businesses. There are numerous "guerrilla" books and websites, such as www.gmarketing.com.

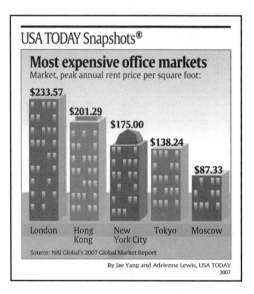

USA TODAY Snapshots®

Most expensive office markets
Market, peak annual rent price per square foot:
$233.57 London
$201.29 Hong Kong
$175.00 New York City
$138.24 Tokyo
$87.33 Moscow
Source: NAI Global's 2007 Global Market Report
By Jae Yang and Adrienne Lewis, USA TODAY 2007

Unlike traditional marketing, which requires money, guerrilla marketing usually requires only time, energy, and imagination. Levinson is a proponent of simple marketing devices such as brochures, signs, classified advertising, and low-cost public events—for example, seminars, free samples, consultations, and product demonstrations. He emphasizes keeping existing customers and getting them to make more transactions. As for your competition, Levinson recommends that you look for ways to cooperate for greater profits—for example, joining together to buy supplies at lower rates or creating a referral system.

Marketing Tip #5: Marketing Is a Sensory Experience

Marketing is a lot like dating. You're trying to get somebody interested and then retain that interest while you continue to sell yourself. And much of the attraction is based on sensory experience—how your business looks, how it smells, and the sense of order that it instills. Don't underestimate the marketing importance of cleanliness and a sense of order (a clutter-free environment) in your home office, vehicle, and personal appearance. Keep in mind that these principles of cleanliness and lack of clutter also apply to your website.

USA TODAY Snapshots®

Small-business owners want better customer service skills

Which business skills would you like to develop further? Top responses:

Customer service **63%**

Marketing/sales **58%**

Financial management **48%**

Decision making **40%**

Negotiation **30%**

Note: Multiple responses allowed
Source: OPEN from American Express Small Business Monitor survey of 625 small-business owners with fewer than 100 employees. Margin of error ±4 percentage points.

By Jae Yang and Veronica Salazar, USA TODAY 2007

Marketing Tip #6: Yes, the Customer Is (Almost) Always Right

Did you know that 80% of complaining customers are unhappier after they complain? Because your customers are your best marketing team, it's crazy to lose them through poor service. One of the least expensive, most effective marketing techniques is to adopt customer-friendly policies. Your customer service program may include response cards, listening without interruption as customers complain, or providing "extras" for customers.

Marketing Tip #7: The Four Marketing Motivators

In *Direct Mail Copy That Sells* (Prentice Hall), Herschel Gordon Lewis describes the commonly known four major marketing motivators: fear, guilt, greed, and exclusivity.

How do they work? Fear is an appeal to whatever the consumer is afraid of—for example, a computer virus, a missed opportunity, auto problems. Gordon thinks that fear, by far, is the greatest motivator, but it works as a marketing motivator only if the customer is provided with a solution to whatever is feared.

Guilt is used to bring back customers who haven't used your services in a while or haven't renewed your newsletter ("we hate losing you …"). Greed is simple—the customer wants to come out ahead ("Here's a special discount we're making only to existing customers"). And exclusivity is the sense of getting something others can't (American Express Platinum card, anyone?).

These motivators may be popular on Madison Avenue, but for side business owners who do not mount major ad campaigns, this manipulative approach may backfire. Fear, for example, may scare off buyers. Guilt may cause customers to avoid your business. Greed and exclusivity may offend. Marketing that's based on quality, not manipulation, is always more effective at creating long-lasting customer relations.

Marketing Tip #8: Use Words That Sell

Did you know there are 62 ways to say "exciting" and 57 ways to say "reliable"? If you can't afford to hire a professional copywriter for your signs, yellow pages ads, product labels, and so forth, then buy a copy of Richard Bayan's *Words That Sell* (McGraw-Hill). It's functional, helpful, and easy to use. The book has five sections—Grabbers, Descriptions & Benefits, Clinchers, Terms & Offers, and Special Strategies—and is a great way to jump-start your advertising and sign copy.

Marketing Tip #9: Don't Rely on Market Research

Market research involves asking questions of people, observing customer behavior, comparing your customers to those of your competitors, talking to ex-customers who have abandoned you, and examining the demographics of your market. But according to Jim Nelens in *Research to Riches: The Secret Rules of Successful Marketing* (Longstreet Press), you'll always get different conclusions depending on the techniques used. For example, questioning people over the phone often produces different results than questioning the same people in person at the mall; questioning people in the morning produces different results than in the evening. Similarly, you'll get a higher response to a mail survey from older people than from younger ones. Before you conduct research—and particularly if you're thinking of hiring a market research company—check out Nelens' book.

Can a Side Business Have a Brand?

You may think that your side business has nothing in common with major brands such as Harley Davidson, Virgin, Nike, or Ben & Jerry's.

Actually, that's not true. A company's acquired "brand" status is not based on extensive advertising and marketing of a name; it evolves from consistently high quality. Brand loyalty means that consumers love what you do. Modern advertising theorists say that branding is really an emotional relationship between consumer and company.

So if customers love your side business, you've got a brand. "If your hair cutting is attracting so much business you're turning down some heads, you've got a brand as well. When you say, 'I'm going to bring this to Paul the Tailor.' That's great branding, too," says business consultant Alan Weiss. "Like the bar in the old TV show *Cheers*, you want to keep coming back."

Without consistent quality, any brand will topple. For example, Coca-Cola, by many estimates the most valuable brand name in the world, took a dive in sales and stock value when it tinkered with its quality and consistency and introduced New Coke. Similarly, it took years for the Jack-in-the-Box fast food chain to build back consumer trust (and its brand name) after an outbreak of food poisoning in 1993. So even though your business is tiny, keep in mind that the same branding principles apply regardless of the size.

To learn more about branding theories and how you can use their insights to advantage, check out the Branding Blog (www. brandingblog.com) or read the leading book on the subject, *Designing Brand Identity*, by Alina Wheeler (Wiley).

Marketing Tip #10: Measure Results

In the marketing world, "accountability" is the term used to test whether a marketing tool is working. Sometimes it's easy to see if a tool is accountable. For example, after Amazon featured Nolo's *Quicken WillMaker Plus* on its home page, online sales of the product doubled. In other cases—particularly with advertising—it's difficult to determine if the effort is working.

The best way to measure results is to provide a special offer tied to the marketing effort. Whether using television, radio, print, or direct mail, try to provide an offer that's unique to that promotion. That makes it much easier to track effectiveness.

Your Marketing Toolbox

It's easy to pick the right tool when making a home repair. But it's a little trickier when you open your marketing toolbox. Which marketing tools are you comfortable with? Which will fit your budget? Which reflect positively on your business? Which ones really work for you?

Our suggestion: Look through these common marketing strategies and ruminate on your business for a few weeks. If you have employees or co-owners, talk about what might work to attract and keep customers. Start slowly. Avoid a big budget. Be patient. Measure results. And stick with what works.

Samples and Free Offers

Kiehl's, the high-end skin care product retailer, is happy to fill each customer's shopping bag with free samples of new products. Can your business afford to offer something for free—for example, a free cookie with every cake? Giving away something you make is usually an inexpensive marketing gesture that will have customers appreciating the value of your products. Customers never seem to tire of these special offers and gifts.

Free offers can function two ways. You may offer existing customers a bonus—for example, Mudpuppy's Tub & Scrub gives a free dog wash after ten purchases. Or you can use free samples to attract new customers—the marketing strategy exploited with much success by cosmetics giant Estee Lauder.

Personal Letters or Cards

Does your insurance agent send you a birthday or Christmas card? Sometimes these efforts seem cheesy; sometimes they're effective. The key to making successful use of personal letters or cards is, well … making them personal. If possible, avoid preprinted labels and form-letter style notes, and if sending out cards, make sure to add something in your handwriting. For example, a musician I know sends out cards announcing upcoming shows. A few years ago, she began writing personal notes on the cards and noticed that attendance increased substantially. Sending a handwritten card to clients—even if it's just to thank them for their continued business—is a small, memorable touch that can go a long way to maintaining customers and clients.

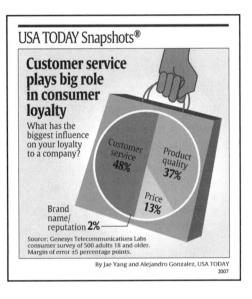

USA TODAY Snapshots®

Customer service plays big role in consumer loyalty

What has the biggest influence on your loyalty to a company?

Customer service **48%**

Product quality **37%**

Price **13%**

Brand name/ reputation **2%**

Source: Genesys Telecommunications Labs consumer survey of 500 adults 18 and older. Margin of error ±5 percentage points.

By Jae Yang and Alejandro Gonzalez, USA TODAY 2007

Telephone Marketing

When you pick up the phone to follow up on sales calls or respond to customer inquiries, you're telemarketing, which is just selling your business over the phone. The stigma attached to telemarketing is associated with cold calls—calling strangers whose phone numbers are provided via a subscription list or through an automatic software dialing device. James Stephenson, author of *Entrepreneur Magazine's Ultimate Small Business Marketing Guide* (Entrepreneur), recommends that you make only "warm calls"—calls to people you know or who you know share common interests. For example, if you teach swimming, can you obtain the membership lists of local swimming clubs? Stephenson also suggests avoiding common telemarketing mistakes—for example, sticking to a script and not listening to what the person on the other end is saying. Also, keep in mind that you are prohibited from calling people who have added their names to the federal Do Not Call Registry (www.donotcall.gov) unless you have an existing business relationship.

Postcards, Handouts, and Brochures

For centuries, small business owners have relied on a relatively inexpensive method of conveying marketing information: cards, brochures, and circulars. For example, you can purchase 1,000 color postcards for your business for less than $200; you can get 1,000 two-page color brochures for $400 to $500. Unfortunately, the value of these marketing efforts is lost unless your printed material expresses the right message both in form and content, and unless you distribute these materials properly— that is, get them into the hands of targeted customers.

In *Guerrilla Marketing* (Houghton Mifflin), Jay Levinson recommends that you focus on one basic idea that you want to express—for example, "We make the most energy-efficient hot tubs" or "We're the most reliable upholsterers"—and then marry that idea with a suitable image. And always include relevant contact information. Two popular and easy-to-use software programs that can assist in your design are Microsoft *Office Publisher* and Broderbund's *Print Shop Deluxe*. Both provide templates for business publications.

Display and Classified Ads

Did you know 61% of Americans read magazines from the back to the front? According to Jay Levinson, that's one indication that an economical classified ad will have a chance for success. Depending on the size and publication, you may spend $20 to $50 for a first insertion. You'll get a frequency discount if you run it three or four times. In addition, many newspapers now run classified ads both in print and online.

Start a Blog: The Ultimate Marketing Tool

Hunting for ways to boost revenue, a growing number of small businesses are adding another weapon to their marketing arsenal: blogging.

A blog lures more traffic to a company's website because it improves chances the site will reach the top of search-engine results. Blogs are easier and cheaper to update than conventional sites. And they encourage customer feedback on new products and services.

What software do I use?

Google and others offer inexpensive, sometimes free, versions, including Blogger, TypePad, Movable Type, and WordPress.

Who contributes to the blog?

The author can be the owner, an employee or several employees. In any case, contributors must write well and—most important—show they care about the company. Consultant Brian Brown estimates that of the 80 small-business blogs he's reviewed, 80% are written by one person, usually the owner.

What should I write about?

A little bit of everything. A restaurant chef could reveal how she created a new dish. A dog trainer might write about a customer's frustrations living with a new puppy.

Good blogs are varied in subject and length of entries. "It's this crazy idea that maybe you should talk to your customers like your friends," says Andy Wibbels, author of *Blogwild!*

How often should I write?

A new entry, or "post," each day would be terrific. If that's too ambitious, Brown recommends at least three posts a week. Sites with lots of pages and many incoming and outgoing links are more likely to appear near the top of search-engine results.

 "Blogs put businesses on Web search map; They help sites reach top of results," by Jim Hopkins, September 20, 2006.

Display ads—boxed advertisements that appear in the body of a newspaper or magazine—are more expensive and vary widely in price. To get the rates, ask for the publication's advertising card. There is also a variation, known as a classified display ad—it runs in the classified ad section—which is less expensive than a regular display ad. What size ad should you run? According to studies, one-quarter of readers notice display ads that occupy a quarter or half a page; 40% notice full-page ads.

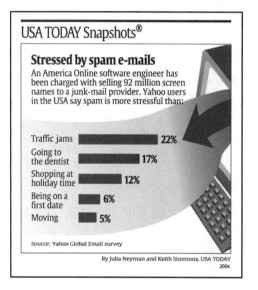

USA TODAY Snapshots®

Stressed by spam e-mails

An America Online software engineer has been charged with selling 92 million screen names to a junk-mail provider. Yahoo users in the USA say spam is more stressful than:

Traffic jams — 22%
Going to the dentist — 17%
Shopping at holiday time — 12%
Being on a first date — 6%
Moving — 5%

Source: Yahoo Global Email survey

By Julia Neyman and Keith Simmons, USA TODAY
2004

Because display ads are often lost in a sea of similar display advertisements, you should take a cautious approach when buying ad space. One of the key elements to a successful display ad campaign is placing the ad in the right publication. Try out one or two different ads as a test and target ads—for example, if you are seeking business-to-business customers, advertise in trade publications; if you are seeking tourist business, advertise in local publications aimed at visitors. As with all your advertising, your message must be succinct and convincing. If possible, log responses to the advertisement to measure its effectiveness.

Yellow Pages

Despite the continuing growth of the Internet, a large number of consumers still use the local telephone company's yellow pages. Over 70% of the respondents in one survey had used the directory to contact a local firm, and half of them had made a purchase. If you place a yellow pages ad, emphasize your specialties, include as much access information as you can, and avoid being cute or too arty—keep in mind that this is an advertisement that will be consulted for at least a year. Compare what your competitors are doing and, as always, track responses, test new ads, and modify when necessary.

Direct Mail

With the advent of the Internet, you might think that direct mail would be dying off, replaced by email advertisements. Not so. According to Seth Godin in *Permission Marketing* (Simon & Schuster), direct mailings have increased in recent years, primarily because they are more effective at "interrupting" consumers than advertisements, and their success rate is measurable.

If you're considering direct mail, though, the response statistics are not good. It's often difficult for a side business owner to compete with the big-buck marketers who are content with a response rate as low as five per thousand mailings (0.5%).

To give your direct mailings an edge, Alexander Hiam, author of *Marketing for Dummies* (Wiley), recommends that you always include three elements:

- bait—something that captures the reader's attention
- the argument—why your product or service can solve a problem for the reader, and
- a call to action—an appeal for immediate action.

In direct mail lingo, these three elements are known as the star, the chain, and the hook. Hiam also recommends that considerable effort be devoted to the envelope so that it announces a special offer or benefit or is artistically creative enough to get the recipient to open it.

How do you create your direct mail address list? If you're interested in setting up a database of existing customers, you'll need software such as Microsoft *Access* or *FileMaker Pro*.

Do you want to send your mailings to strangers? Most likely, you will be best served by sending to existing customers. But if you wish to buy a mailing list, contact one of the many companies that sell or rent them to small business owners (the largest of which is www.infousa.com). For more information on creating successful direct mail, read *Direct Mail Copy That Sells*, by Herschel Gordon Lewis (Prentice Hall).

Also, don't forget email. Although you'll likely want to avoid the stigma of unsolicited email—unaffectionately known as spam—you may find that email blasts to existing customers can effectively alert them to special sales or bonus offers.

Radio and Television

For side-business owners, radio and TV can pose so many problems (and costs) that it's probably not worth pursuing. First, you must target your advertisement so that you're reaching the right listeners or viewers. Second, you must allot quite a bit of your ad marketing budget to produce radio and television advertising. (You'll pay $1,000 to $20,000 per minute for video production, depending on the quality.) Third, more than other forms of advertising discussed in this chapter, radio and TV ads require that you develop a style or an angle—for example, humorous, real-life, educational—and that you engage listeners or viewers for 15 to 60 seconds of air time. Finally, the expense and uncertainty of their effectiveness make radio and TV ads an unlikely marketing tool for penny-pinching side-business owners.

If you are set on proceeding with radio or TV ads, avoid committing to long contracts until you are satisfied with the initial results. Consider using an ad agency to create or place your radio or TV ads—it may give your business a more professional appearance and can sometimes buy airtime at better rates.

Trade Shows

For many side business owners—especially those in a business-to-business market—trade shows are a key marketing tool. It's at the trade show that you meet the sales people and retailers. There are two important variables in trade show marketing: your choice of show and your booth.

You can find trade show listings for your industry in a trade publication, at industry websites, or by using the search feature at the Ultimate Trade Show Resource (www.tsnn.com). If possible, learn about the previous show. You may be able to do this by questioning participants or checking online. For example, attendees at crafts shows often comment on the shows at the message board on *The Crafts Report* magazine website. It's silly to invest in a show if the floors were empty last year.

As for your booth, your initial goal is to get a decent location on the floor and to have a suitable booth size. Get the biggest booth you can afford and invest in a proper display. For information about getting a suitable preassembled booth, type "trade show booth" into a search engine. If cash is really tight, consider sharing a booth with a related business.

Public Relations

How often have you stopped to read a restaurant review posted in a window or a framed article posted in a waiting room? That's public relations at work. The advantages of public relations, as Jay Levinson explains in *Guerrilla Marketing* (Prentice Hall), are that it's free, it provides instant credibility for your business, and it has staying power—you can use reprints as part of a business brochure, for example.

There are two challenges in using this tool: You need to come up with ways to turn your business into news, and you need contacts at local media who will listen to your pitch.

Marketing experts have many suggestions for generating news stories. Jay Levinson recommends connecting your business with something that's in the news right now. Nolo, the publisher of this book, relies heavily on this approach. When news stories appear that relate to the subject of one of its books, a company rep will contact the media to let them know that an expert is

USA TODAY Snapshots®

Small-business marketing costs questionable

When you spend money on marketing, do you see a direct uptick in business/sales?

Yes
46%

No
45%

Not sure
9%

Source: Open from American Express Fall Small Business Monitor survey of 627 small-business owners/managers of companies with fewer than 100 employees. Margin of error: ±4 percentage points.

By Jae Yang and Alejandro Gonzalez, USA TODAY
2007

available to discuss the matter. The important thing is that you fulfill the reporter's primary requirement: an angle or a hook that makes the story interesting to readers. Here are a few suggestions:

- Hold a contest, race, or competitive event and announce the winner.
- Tie in your business with a holiday.
- Sponsor nonprofit activities—for example, sponsor a public performance.
- Become a source of expert information.

How do you get the story to the media? Commonly, it's done with a press release that you send to selected media. (To see examples, check out www.prnewswire.com.) Alexander Hiam has some recommendations when drafting press releases. In particular:

- Try to include lists of tips, rules, or principles.
- Offer yourself as an expert on the industry.
- Keep it short (one page).
- Send it to every editor in the area.
- Post your release on the Web.

Here's one other fact to consider: It's possible that if you buy ad space, you're more likely to get editorial space. Though rarely the case in quality media publications, it's not uncommon in less scrupulous local newspapers or magazines.

Online Advertising

Banner ads, keyword buying, and marketing links? These marketing strategies may work for your business just as they have worked for companies such as Netflix and University of Phoenix Online. For more on how these types of online ads are implemented (and whether they're worth pursuing), see Chapter 2.

Seminars and Product Demonstrations

In *Marketing Without Advertising*, authors Phillips and Rasberry maintain that seminars and demonstrations add vitality to a business and provide value to customers. This type of presentation may be a class—for example, cooking lessons at a kitchen supply store—or you may want to demonstrate a product or service. For example, if you offer framing services, ask a local photography club to let you demonstrate how to best preserve photographs.

Signs

Don't forget about signs. As Paco Underhill points out in *Why We Buy: The Science of Shopping*, if people purchased only the items that triggered their trip to the stores, the retail industry would collapse. What convinces consumers to load the cart and make impulse purchases are signs outside and within a business. It's estimated that new signs inside or outside a business can boost revenue 4% to 8% annually for retailers. Signs work best if they're bold, professionally done, in good condition, consistent with your business, well lit, and tell the viewer your message quickly.

And signs don't just mean words on paper or cardboard. T-shirts, shopping bags, and bumper stickers are also signs and can do a swell job of advertising your goods to the general public.

Outdoor Advertising

What about large outdoor signs like billboards? Considering current traffic statistics, you probably get a decent number of exposures (number of viewers) for outdoor advertising. But the cost is prohibitive—between $3,000 and $5,000 per month to rent a billboard. A less expensive— between $500 and $1,500 per month—way to reach people with outdoor advertising is to purchase transit advertising, such as shelter panels at bus stops or bus posters.

Do You Need a Marketing Plan?

A marketing plan establishes how you're going to spend time and money in promoting your business. Your plan can be professional or informal.

A professional plan usually includes an analysis of your market, the demographics of your customers, your target markets, how you'd like to be positioned within the market, an analysis of your competition, past attempts at marketing and their success rates, and your current strategy and its expenses.

This kind of plan—with its charts and breakdowns of expenditures—is sometimes used as an adjunct for a business plan or as a discrete means of convincing others to invest in your business. If you'd like to create a professional marketing plan, we suggest you invest in *Marketing Plan Pro* from Palo Alto Software (approximately $170), software that enables you to construct a professional marketing plan within a few hours. It includes more than 70 sample plans for various small businesses.

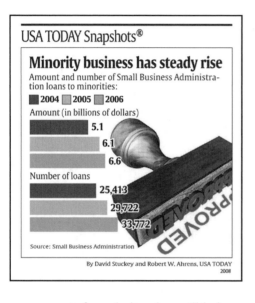

USA TODAY Snapshots®

Minority business has steady rise

Amount and number of Small Business Administration loans to minorities:

■ 2004 ■ 2005 ■ 2006

Amount (in billions of dollars)

5.1
6.1
6.6

Number of loans

25,413
29,722
33,772

Source: Small Business Administration

By David Stuckey and Robert W. Ahrens, USA TODAY 2008

More likely, you won't need to prepare a professional marketing plan. Instead, you may want to try an informal plan that will help you organize your ideas on how to maximize your time and budget.

Start by examining your market. Create a list of current customers. You can probably do this by gathering names from checks, credit card statements, emails, and so forth. Those are your initial and direct targets. Next, determine your potential market using the primary and secondary marketing research techniques. Sometimes, in these cases, it helps to also define the total market—how many total customers is it possible to attract, and what size market share do you want (and can handle)? For example, what percentage of a community of 14,000 households is likely to need dry cleaning services? If you coach high school swimmers, how many competitive student swimmers are there within a 20-mile radius of your training center?

Marketing Tools	
Inexpensive and Worth a Try	**Cost**
Samples and free offers	
Personal letters	
Telephone marketing	
Postcards, handouts, and brochures	
Yellow pages	
Signs	
Seminars, consultations, and demonstrations	
Public relations	
Product demonstrations	
Might Be Worth It	**Cost**
Classified ads	
Online advertising	
Trade shows	
Direct mail	
Display ads	
When You've Got More Money	**Cost**
Radio ads	
Television ads	
Outdoor advertising	

The purpose of your plan is to pick and choose among your marketing tools so that your marketing efforts match your budget. Your budget should be enough to reach your market without cutting seriously into your operating revenues. If you can afford it, start by allocating a percentage—say, 10% of your revenue.

Once you know how much you're prepared to spend on marketing, you must choose your tools and estimate the costs over the year. For example, if you create brochures and handouts, take that one-time cost and spread it over the year ($1,200 for four-color brochures = $100 per month).

This is not a simple task, and the resulting budget is not static. Marketing requires monitoring. It's a process of innovation and change; you abandon or modify tools that aren't working and add and test new ones. Consider your marketing plan as a work in progress.

To help you manage your budget, the table above lists the common elements in a marketing toolbox. ●

Taxes and Deductions

What if we told you that you could save 15% or more on every purchase you make for your side business? What if we told you that you could lower your taxes by deducting side-business losses from your other (nonside-business) income? What if we told you that preparing taxes for your side business has never been easier?

Well, we're telling you.

In this chapter, we focus on three things: paying your taxes, claiming deductions, and understanding the distinction between a hobby and a business—a distinction that can save you a great deal of money at tax time.

What's the Difference? Hobby vs. Business

If you treat your side business as a business, you can deduct your losses from all your income, including your salary, your spouse's income, or interest and investment income. That's a big benefit. You can also carry over deductions from year to year.

If you treat your side business as a hobby, you can deduct your expenses from your hobby income *only*. So if you lose $5,000 on your eBay hobby, you can't deduct it from your other income. This is the "hobby loss rule." And a hobbyist can't carry over deductions to use them in future years when income starts rolling in; they're lost forever.

How the IRS Judges Your Business

So, if you want to claim the maximum tax benefits, you need to meet the IRS standards for a business. The key to meeting this standard is to demonstrate that your primary motive is to earn a profit and that you continuously and regularly engage in your business over a substantial period of time. Here are the IRS rules:

- If you earned a profit from your business in any three of the last five years, the IRS presumes it is a business and is unlikely to question you about it.

- If you didn't earn a profit in any three of the last five years, you will have to show that you behave as if you want to earn a profit (explained in the next section).

When Do You Have a Profit?

You have a profit when the taxable income from an activity is more than the deductions for it—that is, you are not claiming a loss. There is no set amount or percentage of profit you need to earn to satisfy the IRS.

Proving a Profit Motive

If you're audited and you can't show a profit, the IRS will still consider your enterprise a business if you can prove you are guided by a profit motive. The IRS measures your profit motive by looking at five "business behavior" factors. Studies show that taxpayers who satisfy the first three factors—you act like you're in business, you demonstrate expertise, and you show time and effort expended—are routinely classified as businesses even if they don't expect to profit for years.

- **Act like you're in business.** Keeping good books and other records goes a long way to show that you carry on activities in a businesslike manner. For example, husband and wife sculptors were able to claim business losses by providing records of exhibits at museums and galleries and testimonials to their skill and sales potential from art experts. (*Rood v. U.S.*, 184 F. Supp. 791 (D. Minn. 1960).)

- **Acquire expertise within your industry.** It helps to show that you're industry savvy. For example, an inventor developed a miles-per-gallon indicator but gave up on it after learning that General Motors was developing something similar. The tax court found a profit motive in the inventor's decision to drop the project; it showed he was savvy enough to realize he couldn't compete against GM. (*Maximoff v. Commissioner*, T.C. Memo 1987-155.)

- **Work regularly.** The IRS is looking for proof that you work regularly and continuously, not sporadically, on your side business. What's "regularly and continuously"? One court accepted 20 to 30 hours per week (*Maximoff v. Commissioner*, T.C. Memo 1987-155); another accepted 25 hours per week for three years, then five to ten hours per week for two years (*Luow v. Commissioner*, T.C. Memo 1971-326). When a taxpayer couldn't establish the time spent, a court called it a hobby (*Everson v. Commissioner*, 2001 TNT 115-8).

- **Establish a record.** Having a record of success in other businesses in the past—whether or not they are related to your current business—creates the likelihood that your activities are a business.

- **Earn some profits.** Even if you can't satisfy the three-out-of-five-years profit test, earning a profit one year after years of losses helps show you are in a business.

USA TODAY Snapshots®

Two lengthy codes
Number of pages in:

King James Bible **1,472**

U.S. tax code **20,000**

Sources: Amazon.com and Internal Revenue Service

By David Stuckey and Adrienne Lewis, USA TODAY 2005

The IRS is skeptical of taxpayers who claim large business losses from their side businesses, but who have substantial income from other sources. And, unfairly or not, the IRS may also doubt your motives if you're having lots of fun with your side business. Deductions for a snowboarding business will raise more red flags than deductions for a graphics business. That's not to say you can't have fun in your business. Here are two examples:

- **Here comes speedy.** After 20 years in sales and market research, Robert decided to turn his passion—gambling at the dog track—into his business. When the IRS questioned him about it, he was able to show that he had spent 60 to 80 hours each week for 48 weeks either at dog tracks or at home studying racing forms, programs, and other materials. Even though his efforts generated a net gambling loss of $2,032, the U.S. Supreme Court ruled that Robert was engaged in a business. (*Commissioner of Internal Revenue v. Groetzinger*, 480 U.S. 23 (1987).)

- **Deducting her derailleur.** Donna, a customer service manager for a sporting goods company, had a side business competing in bicycle races. When the IRS questioned her, she demonstrated her expertise and documented her diligence in pursuing her goal: She raced 30 times a year, trained daily, and had sponsors who provided bicycles, clothing, and, occasionally, entry fees. Even though she incurred expenses that exceeded her racing income, the court ruled that bicycle racing was her business. (*In re Fletcher*, 248 B.R. 48 (*Bankr. D. Vt.*, 2000).)

Classic Hobby Loss Abuse

To give you an idea of some of the extreme abuse the IRS is looking to stop, here are two classics:

- **The 27-year search for the perfect steak.** When Maurice wasn't in the Canary Islands living off a family trust, he traveled the world sampling food and wines. For 20 years, he gathered material for his book, *My 27-Year Search for the Perfect Steak—Still Looking.* Two publishers rejected the book, and he abandoned plans for publication. Maurice claimed that the book was part of his bid to create a business around his "multimedia personality." He claimed losses of approximately $22,000 and $28,000 for two years. The IRS disallowed the deductions because Maurice couldn't show any evidence he was working towards his multimedia personality goal or that he had an expectation of profit. (*Dreicer v. Commissioner*, 78 T.C. 642, 1982 U.S. Tax Ct. LEXIS 109, 78 T.C. No. 44 (1982).)

- **How to heat a palm tree.** Martin, a wealthy inventor and manufacturer of farm implements, decided to build a luxury house with swimming pool and tennis courts. The house had some creative features—there was no wood used in the construction, only glass, plastic, and aluminum; there were motorized drapes, an automatic watering system for the lawn, and even a palm tree with a warming coil in the planter. In a creative accounting effort, he deducted the cost of his new home from his income, calling it experimentation for his inventing business and claiming that he planned to exploit the home's innovations. The tax court wasn't persuaded. Apparently, Martin had not done any research before commencing the costly construction to determine if a market existed for the innovations he had in mind, and he didn't keep any records during the construction process so that he could later commercially apply these innovations. He had moved his family into the house immediately upon completion and apparently forgot about taking any further steps towards profiting on his "housing experiments" until three years later—at about the same time that the Internal Revenue Service was auditing his income tax returns. (*Mayrath v. Commissioner*, 357 F.2d 209 (5th Cir. 1966).)

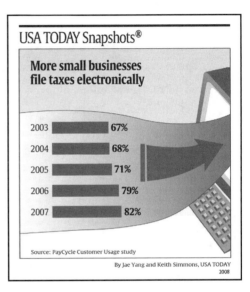

USA TODAY Snapshots®

More small businesses file taxes electronically

2003	67%
2004	68%
2005	71%
2006	79%
2007	82%

Source: PayCycle Customer Usage study

By Jae Yang and Keith Simmons, USA TODAY 2008

If you need more assistance wrestling with the hobby loss rule, check out the small-business owners section of the IRS website at www.irs.gov/businesses/small/index.html.

Who Doesn't Pay Their Taxes?

Small-business owners are the biggest source of uncollected taxes, the IRS says.

Restaurants may use sales tax collections to cover rent, rather than pass them on to the government as required. A construction company may make payroll first and worry about taxes later.

Once on the slippery slope, it's hard to recover because penalties and interest are severe.

Jim Armstrong of Marysville, Washington, sells prefabricated industrial buildings. In 2003, he delayed paying $330,000 in sales taxes, waiting for a big check at the end of a job. The check never arrived.

"We got stiffed," he says. He expected $1 million and got $200,000 in mediation.

That money went to the tax collector, but it wasn't enough.

He now owes $404,899 in taxes, interest and penalties. The meter is running every day. And last month, the state cleaned out two of his wife's checking accounts.

Armstrong, 64, says he was once a millionaire. Now, he's struggling to rebuild a business.

Washington Revenue Department spokesman Mike Gowrylow says he can't talk about a specific case, but "we bend over backward to work with businesses."

He adds: "Remember, sales tax isn't a tax on the business. It's a tax the business collected from someone else, kept and did not remit to the state."

Armstrong says that "I'm the first one to admit we did something we weren't supposed to do. We've tried to repay at tremendous personal hardship."

 "Tax delinquents encounter varying outcomes," by Dennis Cauchon, April 14, 2008.

Paying Taxes

Preparing and paying taxes for your side business is more complicated than paying your taxes when you work as someone else's employee. You'll have plenty of new tax forms to complete, new rules to follow, and strategic decisions to make. The good news is that you can easily tackle your new paperwork using a Web-based or software tax preparation program, once you know your obligations.

The basic formula for paying tax on a side business is the same as paying tax on a salary or other sources of income. You pay tax on your net income—the money you earn less your deductions. As the owner of a side business, however, you have some additional tax obligations.

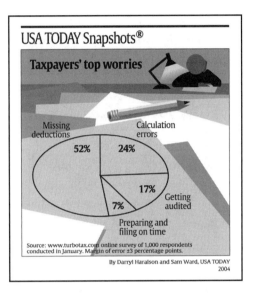

USA TODAY Snapshots®

Taxpayers' top worries

Missing deductions 52%
Calculation errors 24%
Getting audited 17%
Preparing and filing on time 7%

Source: www.turbotax.com online survey of 1,000 respondents conducted in January. Margin of error ±3 percentage points.

By Darryl Haralson and Sam Ward, USA TODAY 2004

For example, you have to pay self-employment taxes, which fund your Social Security and Medicare contributions. It gets more complicated if you have employees, because you'll have to pay part of their Social Security and Medicare payments, pay federal unemployment tax, and withhold (and periodically send to the government) income tax from your employees. And you'll probably have to pay your income taxes in four installments throughout the year, rather than all at once on April 15.

Will You Get Audited?

These days, most people who disobey tax rules have a good chance of escaping the IRS's clutches—generally only between 1% and 1.2% of taxpayers are audited each year. Most of these audits are triggered by a computer analysis known as the discriminate function system (or DIF), which looks for red flags in a tax return. Several factors arouse suspicion:

- The individual filing has substantial assets.
- The deduction is very high, perhaps tens of thousands of dollars.
- The business is one that could be considered a leisure experience—such as horse breeding or yacht charters.

When suspicious factors light up, the odds of being selected by the DIF system increase. However, be aware that every once in a while, the IRS breaks from this pattern and selects an otherwise unlikely candidate for audit.

How Businesses Are Taxed

How you pay taxes on your business profits will depend on how you have structured your side business. If you're like the hundreds of thousands of other side-business operators, you're likely operating as a single-owner sole proprietorship. If you're operating with someone else, you're most likely a partnership. If you're concerned with personal liability, you may have formed a limited liability company (LLC) or corporation.

For tax purposes, however, there are only two categories of business taxpayers: those who pay tax on business income on their individual tax returns (called pass-through entities, because income and expenses pass through the business to the owner) and those who must pay their own taxes.

Most likely, you are a pass-through entity. Sole proprietorships, partnerships, LLCs, and S corporations (corporations that elect to be taxed like partnerships) are all pass-through entities. A pass-through entity does not pay its own taxes. Instead, its profits or losses pass through to the owners, who must report those amounts on their personal tax returns.

Here are the basic rules:

- **Sole proprietors** report business income and expenses on IRS Schedule C, *Profit or Loss From Business*, which they have to file along with their personal tax returns (IRS Form 1040).

- **Partners** report their share of partnership income and expenses on IRS Schedule E, *Supplemental Income and Loss*, which they must file along with their 1040s. In addition, the partnership itself must file an informational return (IRS Form 1065, *U.S. Return of Partnership Income*) and provide each partner with an IRS Schedule K-1, *Partner's Share of Income, Credits, Deductions, etc.*, which lists each partner's share of income and expenses.

- **Shareholders in S corporations** report income and expenses on their personal tax returns (IRS Schedule C, *Profit or Loss From Business*, and IRS Form 1040). In addition, the S corporation must file IRS Form 1120S, *U.S. Income Tax Return for an S Corporation*. This return gives the IRS information, but you don't use it to figure tax owed.

- **LLC members** report their income and expenses just like sole proprietors if they have one-member LLCs. In a multimember LLC, members report their income and expenses, just like partners. A multimember LLC also has to file IRS Form 1065, *U.S. Return of Partnership Income* and issue an IRS Schedule K-1 to each member. (LLCs may, however, choose to be taxed as C corporations by filing IRS Form 8832, *Entity Classification Election*.)

- **Shareholders in C corporations** differ from their business brethren because the C corporation is the only business form that is not a pass-through entity. A C corporation must file its own tax return and pay its own taxes on corporate income. (It does so by filing IRS Form 1120, *U.S. Corporation Income Tax Return*.) Corporate shareholders have to pay personal income tax (on the 1040) only on any business income paid out to them as compensation or dividends. This is where the potential tax-saving benefits of incorporating come from: Because shareholders can decide how much corporate income to distribute and how much to retain in the corporation, they can allocate most of the money to the taxpayer with the lowest rates—usually, the corporation.

	How Businesses Report Income		
Type of business	Owner pays tax on personal tax return	Business pays tax itself	Business must file its own tax return
Sole proprietor	x		
Partnership	x		x
One-member LLC	x		
Multimember LLC	x		x
S corporation	x		x
C corporation		x	x

What Taxes Your Business Will Have to Pay

There are three basic types of taxes a typical self-employed businessperson might have to pay: income taxes, self-employment taxes, and employment taxes. In addition, if you sell goods or services on which your state imposes a sales tax, you will have to collect this money and periodically hand it over to your state taxing authority.

Income taxes. You will have to pay income taxes on the net profit your side business earns. The federal government imposes an income tax, as do the governments of most states. Some local governments also get into the act by taxing businesses within their jurisdictions; a few use an income tax, while others use some other method (an inventory, payroll, or business equipment tax, for example). (If you live in Alaska, Florida, Nevada, South Dakota, Texas, Washington, and Wyoming, you already know that these states don't impose income taxes.)

Self-employment taxes. You are responsible for paying your own Social Security and Medicare taxes. Unlike employees, whose employers are legally required to chip in for half of these amounts, you will have to pay the entire bill—currently, a 12.4% Social Security tax and a 2.9% Medicare tax on all of your taxable income from self-employment.

However, you are entitled to deduct half of these taxes from your gross income for purposes of calculating your income tax, so the total effective self-employment tax rate is about 12%. To report and pay self-employment taxes, you must file IRS Form SE, *Self-Employment Tax*, along with your annual tax return.

Employment taxes. In the event you have employees, you will have to pay half of their Social Security and Medicare taxes, as well as unemployment tax and perhaps temporary disability tax (to your state taxing authority). You'll also have to withhold taxes from your employees' paychecks and deposit them with the IRS. To report and pay unemployment tax, you file IRS Form 940, *Employer's Annual Federal Unemployment Tax (FUTA) Tax Return*. To report all withholdings and pay your share of Social Security and Medicare, you must file IRS Form 941, *Employer's Quarterly Federal Tax Return*. The rules for employment taxes can get pretty tricky, and many employers are required to make quarterly filings with the IRS. For more information, check out IRS Publication 15 (Circular E), *Employer's Tax Guide* (you can get it at www.irs.gov).

Sales tax. Almost every state has a sales tax. You're undoubtedly used to paying sales tax as a consumer, but now that you're in business, you'll be on the other end of the transaction: You'll be responsible for collecting sales tax from your customers and paying that money to the state. State sales tax rules vary considerably: Some states tax only sales of goods, while others also tax services; in every state, certain sales are exempt from tax (that is, you don't have to collect or pay tax on the sale), but every state's list of exempt transactions is different, and states have different rules

USA TODAY Snapshots®

States with the most business-friendly tax climate

South Dakota | Florida | Alaska | Texas | New Hampshire

Note: Rankings were based on five factors: Low or no corporate income tax, low or no individual income tax, no or low sales tax, least complex unemployment insurance tax and the ability to raise sufficient tax revenue without a corporate, individual or sales tax.
Source: Tax Foundation 2004 State Business Tax Climate Index

By Darryl Haralson and Alejandro Gonzalez, USA TODAY 2005

about when and how you must submit the tax you collect to the state taxing authority. To find the rules in your state, your best bet is to go straight to your state tax agency for help (you can find a list of links at www.irs.gov). You can also get a lot of good basic information, as well as details about every state's sales tax scheme, at www.toolkit.cch.com (look under "Controlling Your Taxes" in the Small Business Guide).

Paying Estimated Taxes

Your side-business clients and customers don't withhold taxes from what they pay you. This is a financial advantage for you; you not only receive the full amount you are owed, but also have greater freedom to plan your finances. The IRS is not so enthusiastic, however; it wants to get your tax dollars right away, rather than waiting for you to pay the whole tab on April 15.

That's why self-employed people have to pay estimated taxes—taxes on their estimated annual incomes, paid in four installments over the course of each year. These payments must include both estimated income tax and estimated self-employment taxes.

Estimated Tax Payment Schedule	
Income received	**Estimated tax due**
January 1 through March 31	April 15
April 1 through May 31	June 15
June 1 through August 31	September 15
September 1 through December 31	January 15 of the following year

You don't have to pay estimated taxes until you earn some income. For example, if your business doesn't bring in any income by March 31, you don't have to make an estimated tax payment on April 15.

Not everyone has to pay estimated taxes. You don't if:

- You expect to owe less than $1,000 in federal tax for the year.

- You paid no taxes last year, if you were a U.S. citizen and your tax return covered the full 12-month period.

- Your business is a C corporation and you receive dividends or distributions of profits from your corporation on which you will owe less than $500 in tax for the year. (You don't have to pay estimated taxes on salary you receive from your corporation; instead, you report that income and pay tax on it annually, on your personal tax return.)

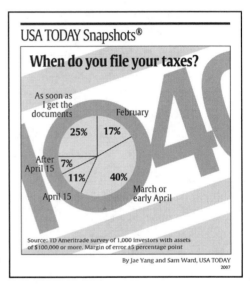

USA TODAY Snapshots®

When do you file your taxes?

As soon as I get the documents: 25%

February: 17%

March or early April: 40%

April 15: 11%

After April 15: 7%

Source: TD Ameritrade survey of 1,000 investors with assets of $100,000 or more. Margin of error ±5 percentage point

By Jae Yang and Sam Ward, USA TODAY 2007

But even if you don't have to pay estimated taxes, you might want to do it anyway. Paying estimated taxes spreads your tax bill over the entire year, so you won't have to come up with all of the money at once. On the other hand, as long as you really have enough socked away to cover your bill, paying it all at once will give you the benefit of that money—and its interest-earning power—for a longer period of time.

There are three ways to figure out how much estimated tax to pay. The easiest method is to simply pay exactly what you owed in federal tax the previous year (or a bit more, if you earned more than $150,000). However, if you don't expect to owe as much this year, you may want to look into the second and third methods listed below; although they are more complicated, they could result in a lower tax bill.

- **Pay what you paid last year.** To use this method, simply divide your total federal tax payments for the previous year by four, then pay that amount when estimated taxes are due. (If you earn more than $150,000 annually—$75,000 for married people filing separately—you'll have to pay 110% of your previous year's tax bill.) As long as you pay this amount, you won't owe the IRS any penalties, even if your current year's income is higher and you end up owing more tax at the end of the year.

No Tax Last Year = No Estimated Tax This Year

No matter how much money you earn or how much you expect to owe in federal income and self-employment tax, you have no obligation to pay estimated taxes if you had no tax liability in the previous year. This is true regardless of the discrepancy between this year's and last year's earnings. However, you must have filed a tax return for the previous year in order to take advantage of this rule—and that's true even if your side business is an illegal venture.

For example, after Eddie Lee Williams was convicted of cocaine distribution and money laundering, the IRS went after him for failing to report—and pay estimated taxes on—his drug-related income. (Yes, the government expects people to report income from illegal activities.) Based on Williams's bank records and purchases (including three cars in a single year), the IRS estimated that he earned more than $100,000 in unreported income in 1989, a year for which he never filed a tax return. The tax court found that Williams was liable for failing to file a return and report this income, and that he owed a substantial amount in unpaid income taxes. However, the court refused to find Williams guilty of failing to pay estimated taxes on the income. The reason? Williams and his wife filed a return in 1988, in which they reported only $2,000 in income and for which they owed no tax. Because Williams owed no tax for the previous year, he was not required to make estimated tax payments in 1989, even though his earnings skyrocketed. (*Williams v. Commissioner*, TC Memo 2003-216.)

- **Make payments based on your estimated income.** If you expect to earn less this year than you did last year, you might save money by making tax payments based on this year's estimated taxable income. The catch, of course, is that it can be very tough to estimate income and expenses ahead of time. The IRS knows this, and won't charge you any penalties as long as your estimated payments cover at least 90% of the current year's tax bill (of course, you will have to pay the additional tax). To use this method, estimate your total taxable income for the year, calculate the tax you will owe (don't forget self-employment taxes), and pay one quarter of that amount when each estimated payment falls due.

- **Make payments based on your estimated quarterly income.** Under this method, you calculate your taxable income (including prorated deductions) at the end of each payment period, then pay that amount on the due date. This is probably the toughest method to use, but may be worthwhile if your income fluctuates a lot throughout the year (for example, if your business is intensely seasonal). It allows you to pay little or no estimated tax during your "dry" periods, and save your tax bills for more profitable days.

Preparing Your Taxes

Before you sit down to fill in your tax forms, we advise following a two- (okay, sometimes three-) step process. First, do as much research as necessary so that you can understand the decisions you'll have to make. For example, as we'll explain, you often have a choice of either depreciating a major purchase or deducting its entire cost in the year you buy it. Only you can decide which makes more sense for your business, and you'll probably need to learn more about each option to make the right choice.

The information in this book will give you a jump on your research; for more help, start with Nolo's tax deduction books: *Deduct It!* and *Home Business Tax Deductions*, both by Stephen Fishman.

There are also plenty of great websites that offer free tax information. The best place to start is the IRS website, www.irs.gov. You can find a lot of useful articles and links on its home page for small businesses and the self-employed, and its free publications are loaded with information. You can download your tax forms here, too.

USA TODAY Snapshots®

Who prepares your tax return?

I do my own

59%

41%

I hire a professional

Source: TD Ameritrade survey of 1,000 investors with assets of $100,000 or more. Margin of error ±5 percentage points.

By Jae Yang and Dave Merrill, USA TODAY
2007

Once you are ready to actually prepare your returns, you have a number of options, ranging from filling in the forms yourself to hiring a certified public accountant to do your taxes. Often, the best choice falls in the middle of this range: using a Web-based or software program to complete your tax forms. These programs are cost-effective, can save you a lot of time and stress, and will help you not only complete the forms properly, but also figure out when you need more information to make the right decision.

We strongly recommend using a tax preparation software program. Two programs in particular dominate the field—*Turbotax* and H&R Block *TaxCut*. Both programs use a question-and-answer interview format, so you can simply provide the requested information and count on the program to fill in the appropriate forms. And you can always go back to a previous year's tax return to make instant comparisons and see how your business looks to the IRS over time. If you get stuck on a question or realize that you need to talk to a tax professional before deciding how to respond, you can simply exit the program and pick up where you left off once you have the information you need.

Unreported Income is a No-No

Although many taxpayers fear an audit of their claimed deductions, the IRS is actually much more interested in income than expenses. Unreported income is often the first thing auditors look for, and they will be very suspicious if you have significant deposits beyond the income you claimed on your return, even if those deposits are to your personal account. If you have significant nontaxable income, make sure to keep the records you'll need to prove where it came from.

Don't expect the IRS to take your word for it, especially if you claim that the money belongs to someone else and just happened to find its way into your bank account. Judging from cases decided by the U.S. Tax Court, this is a fairly popular argument that is extremely likely to fail, unless you can show written proof of your claim and it looks like something other than a tax evasion ploy.

Keeping Records for the IRS

If you face an audit, the IRS is not going to be satisfied with anything less than real, tangible proof. You'll have to come up with receipts, cancelled checks, bank statements, and other records to support both the amount of income you claimed and any business deductions you took. You really can throw it all in a shoebox if you want, but most business owners find it easier to use a set of file folders or an accordion file (you can buy one that's already labeled with common business expense categories at an office supply store).

Here's a brief rundown on what you need to keep as proof of income and expenses:

- To document income, you'll need copies of your bank statements, copies of checks you've deposited, copies of any 1099s you received, and, if you have nontaxable income, copies of documents showing the source of that income (for example, from an inheritance). Remember, the IRS is less interested in the business income you reported than in the income it thinks you failed to report. This means your job is not really to prove the amount of income your business earned, but to prove that any income you didn't report came from a nontaxable source.

- To document most business expenses, you must keep records showing what you bought, who you bought it from, how much you paid, and the date of the purchase. In most cases, you can prove this with your receipt and a cancelled check or credit card statement (which proves that the receipt is really yours).

- To document vehicle expenses, keep records of the dates of all business trips, your destination, the business purpose of your trip (for example, to meet with a client or scout a retail location), and your mileage.

- To document meals and entertainment, keep records of what you paid for, who you bought it from, how much you paid, the date of purchase, who you were with, and the business purpose of your meeting. The first four facts are often included on a receipt; the remaining two you can record in a date book or calendar.

- To document your use of property, retain records of how much time you spent using it for business and using it for other purposes. This rule applies to listed property, items that the IRS believes people often use for personal purposes, including computers and cameras. (You can find listed property in IRS Publication 946, *How to Depreciate Property*.) You might also want to keep track of the time you spend in your home office, to prove that you used it regularly. You can keep these records in a log or journal.

We can't say it enough: Don't expect the IRS to allow your tax deductions if you don't keep records to back them up. If you have no records at all, your deductions will be disallowed in an audit, and you might face penalties as well. If you can prove that you had some business-related expenses of a type that makes sense for your line of work, the IRS may still allow a deduction, but it will be much smaller than what you claimed. Under the Cohan rule (named for a tax suit against entertainer George Cohan), if you can show some proof that you incurred deductible expenses, the IRS can estimate those expenses and allow a deduction for that amount. But, as you might expect, the IRS's estimates will be low. And this rule doesn't apply to expenses for travel, vehicles, gifts, and meals and entertainment. The IRS requires more detailed records for these types of deductions.

How Long Should You Keep Records?

In most situations, the IRS has up to three years to audit you after you file a tax return (or after the date when your tax return was due, if you filed early). However, if the IRS claims that you have unreported income exceeding 25% of the income you did report, it has six years to audit you. And if you didn't file a return or the IRS claims that your return was fraudulent, there is no audit deadline; you're always fair game.

Based on these rules, some experts advise that you simply give up and keep all of your tax records forever. We certainly think there's no harm in keeping all of your actual tax returns forever; they don't take up much space and can help you track the financial life of your business over time. The supporting documents are another story. Unless you filed a fraudulent return (and this is something only you can decide), you can generally get rid of supporting documents six years after you file your tax returns.

Donald Teschner, who played guitar, violin, and mandolin in Rod Stewart's band, found himself on the losing end of the Cohan rule. He claimed an employee deduction for stage clothing, including silk boxers and leather pants, but couldn't provide sufficient documentation to back up his claim that these items were required for his work. The court found that he could deduct only clothing so "flashy and loud" that it was not suitable for everyday wear and, further, found that his receipts weren't sufficiently detailed to prove what he spent for flashy items as opposed to regular clothes. However, the court, apparently willing to believe that a musician backing up the man who sings "Do Ya Think I'm Sexy?" has to make some effort to stand out on stage, allowed him $200 of his claimed $695 deduction. (*Teschner v. Commissioner of Internal Revenue*, TC Memo 1997-498.)

Tax Deductions

You probably already know one of the cardinal rules of business: You have to spend money to make money. Fortunately, the government is prepared to give you some of that money back by allowing you to deduct most of what you spend on your side business.

When you consider what a great deal the government is offering, you'll realize how important it is to understand tax deductions. By letting you deduct your expenses, the government is essentially offering to pick up part of the tab for your venture. After you factor in federal income taxes, state income taxes, and self-employment taxes, every dollar you spend on deductible business expenses could save you more than 40 cents on your tax bill. The offer is on the table; it's up to you to take advantage of it by claiming every tax deduction to which you're entitled.

This chapter explains some of the most common deductions. However, once you start racking up deductible expenses, you'll need more information. Nolo offers two great books on the subject: *Deduct It!* and *Home Business Tax Deductions*, both by Stephen Fishman. You can also find a lot of helpful guidance, including publications that explain various types of deductions, at the IRS website, www.irs.gov.

What's a Tax Deduction Worth?

A deduction is the cost or value of something that you can subtract from your gross income (all the money you earn) to determine your taxable income (the amount on which you have to pay tax). It's not a dollar-for-dollar proposition: You don't save the entire amount you paid for deductible goods and services. But because you don't have to pay tax on this amount, a deduction can save you almost half of what you spend.

The exact amount you'll save by taking a deduction depends on your tax bracket—the tax rate that applies to your income. The higher your bracket, the more every deduction is worth.

> **EXAMPLE:** Simon spends $2,000 on a computer for his eBay business. He's in the 25% federal income tax bracket. By deducting the cost of the computer, he doesn't have to pay tax on $2,000 of his income. That saves him 25% of $2,000, or $500. But that's not all. The state where Simon does business imposes a 6% income tax, so Simon saves an additional $120 there. And Simon doesn't have to pay self-employment taxes— the amount self-employed people have to chip in to fund their Social Security and Medicare—on this money, either. The self-employment tax rate works out to about 12%, for an additional $240 savings. Simon ends up saving $860, almost half of what he paid for his computer.

Seven Often-Overlooked Deductions

Many side-business owners miss out on valuable business deductions simply because they don't know which expenses they can deduct. Dan Hoffman, CPA and director of the San Francisco–based accounting firm Lautze & Lautze (www.lautze.com), says that business owners often forget to deduct the following.

Overlooked Deduction #1: Bad Debts

If someone owes your business money and it's starting to look like you're never going to get paid back, you might be able to deduct the amount of the bad debt.

Overlooked Deduction #2: Casualty Losses

If your side-business property is damaged or destroyed by fire, vandalism, flood, or some other sudden, unexpected, or unusual event, you can claim the amount of the loss as a deduction—but only to the extent that the loss isn't covered by insurance.

Overlooked Deduction #3: Dues, Subscriptions, and Fees

Dues or fees you pay to professional organizations—such as a trade association or membership group—are deductible business expenses. So are charges for subscriptions to professional, technical, or trade journals in your field.

Overlooked Deduction #4: Education Expenses

If you buy books, take a college course, or attend a convention to keep up with the latest trends in your field, you can deduct your costs. As long as the expenditure either improves your business-related skills or is required to maintain your career status (for example, you are a caterer and attend a lecture on food and hygiene), it's deductible.

Overlooked Deduction #5: Phone Bills

If you have a separate business line in your home office, you should deduct not only the costs associated with that phone, but also the cost of occasional business calls you make from your cell phone or personal phone line.

Overlooked Deduction #6: Retirement Plans

You can deduct the money you contribute to most types of retirement plans that you set up for yourself or your employees.

Overlooked Deduction #7: Federal and State Tax Credits

Tax credits may be available to businesses that help further particular civic goals—for example, by hiring employees through a welfare-to-work program, doing business in designated "empowerment" or "renewal" zones (communities that are struggling economically), or using solar energy. You can find information on federal credits in IRS Publication 334, *Tax Guide for Small Business*; for information on state credits, contact your state taxing authority.

Postponing Start-Up Costs

If you've already incurred start-up costs, you'll have to follow the rules laid out below. And, if you won't spend more than $5,000 on start-up expenses, you can simply deduct them all at once. However, if you're looking at more than $5,000 in future start-up costs, it's worth taking a couple of steps to avoid having to spread out part of your deduction over the next 15 years.

The key is to start your business before you lay out significant amounts of money; that way, your expenses are usually immediately deductible. If you will offer services, your business starts when you first make your services available to the public, whether or not you actually have any customers. If you'll be making products, you're in business once you start the process, even if you have not yet solicited any sales or completed any products.

Here are two ways to convert what would be start-up costs into immediately deductible business expenses:

- **Postpone major purchases until you're up and running.** Once you hang out your shingle, you can buy that fancy computer system and office furniture, or shell out thousands of dollars for advertising.

- **Postpone paying for purchases.** If you absolutely have to pay for some expensive items or services before you open your doors, buy them on credit (or ask to be billed later). As long as you're a cash-basis taxpayer (you record income when you receive it and expenses when you pay them), you haven't actually incurred an expense until the money leaves your wallet. And as long as you pay the bill after you start up, you'll probably have an immediately deductible expense.

Tax Deduction Basics

How much you can deduct and when you can take the deduction depend on the type of expense. There are four basic categories of deductions, and the rules for each are a bit different.

Start-Up Expenses

Money that you spend before your business is up and running—such as the cost of researching what kind of business to start or advertising your grand opening—are start-up expenses. When it comes to dealing with these expenses, you can:

- **Treat them as part of your basis in the business.** This means that you cannot deduct them, but you can add them in when you calculate the value of your business for purposes of figuring out your capital gain (or loss) when you sell or shut down.
- **Deduct them over time.** You may deduct up to $5,000 of them right away; you must deduct the remainder over the first 180 months you are in business.

Operating Expenses

Once you are in business, your day-to-day costs are operating expenses. These might include money you spend on office rent, employee salaries, travel, professional services, office supplies, advertising, interest on business loans or purchases, and so on. As long as you aren't paying for something that you will use for more than a year (such as a vehicle or computer—see below), you can deduct these expenses in the year when you spend the money. The IRS has created special rules for operating expenses that it believes are often overstated or abused: travel, vehicle, and entertainment expenses. (These are covered in more detail below.)

Capital Expenses

If you buy things for your business that have a useful life of more than one year—like a car, furniture, or machinery—then you have purchased a long-term asset. You usually can choose to depreciate these assets (deducting a portion of the cost for each year of the item's useful life, as determined by the IRS) or deduct them all at once. (See "Deducting Long-Term Assets," below, for more information.)

Inventory

Special rules apply to inventory, the products you make or buy to sell to customers. You must wait until you sell inventory to deduct the cost of making or buying it. This is why so many businesses are desperate to get rid of their inventory at the end of the year: They want to take a larger deduction, and they want to minimize their burden when it comes time to count inventory for tax purposes.

Deducting Home Office Expenses

You probably run your side business from your home and if you do, you may be able to deduct expenses relating to your home workspace. Although commonly referred to as the home office deduction, this deduction actually applies to any home space you use for your side business, including a studio, workshop, or laboratory.

Whether you qualify for a home office deduction, you can always deduct the direct costs of running your side business—for example, if you buy a computer to use in your business, pay for high-speed Internet access to do your work, or use your personal phone for business calls, you may deduct those costs whether or not you claim the home office deduction. But using the home office deduction allows you to claim a portion of

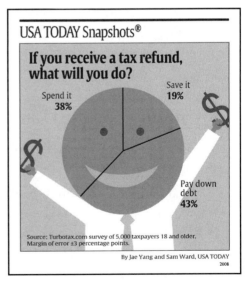

USA TODAY Snapshots®

If you receive a tax refund, what will you do?

Spend it **38%**

Save it **19%**

Pay down debt **43%**

Source: Turbotax.com survey of 5,000 taxpayers 18 and older. Margin of error ±3 percentage points.

By Jae Yang and Sam Ward, USA TODAY 2008

the costs of your home—rent, utility bills, cleaning services, homeowner fees, and so on—as a business expense.

My Three Deductions

If you hire your own children, spouse, parents, or anyone else who might have a legitimate personal claim to your financial support, then you'll have to be ready to prove that they really performed work for you and that it was worth what you paid them.

Don't follow the example of Gary Bybee, who claimed to be working with a team of professionals in his toxic waste disposal business. In fact, his only employees were his three sons, whom he said he hired to do research and read periodicals at their respective universities. He also claimed that, rather than paying them a salary, he found it more convenient to pay for their college tuition and living expenses. Needless to say, the court disallowed his claimed deductions for their travel and home office expenses—in fact, the court found that Bybee wasn't running a business at all. (*Bybee v. Commissioner of Internal Revenue*, 29 F.3d 630 (9th Cir. 1994).)

Qualifying for the Home Office Deduction

To qualify for the home office deduction, you must first satisfy the IRS's threshold test:

- You must use your home workspace regularly and exclusively for your side business (unless you store inventory or run a day care center at home—see below).

- You must use your home workspace exclusively for business, not for personal or other purposes. You don't have to devote an entire room to your business to qualify; you can use a portion of a room as a home office, as long as you use it exclusively for business. If you mix business with pleasure—for example, you use your workspace to correspond with clients and handle business bookkeeping, but also to play online poker and pay household bills—then you won't qualify for the home office deduction.

- You must also use your home office regularly—that is, on a continuing basis, not just for occasional work. The IRS has never clearly explained exactly what it considers regular use. One court found 12 hours a week sufficiently regular, but no one really knows how low you can go.

If you use your home office exclusively and regularly for business, you will qualify for the home office deduction if you meet one of these five additional tests:

- **Your home office is your principal place of business.** If you do all or almost all of your work in your home office, you meet this test. If you work in more than one location, however, you'll have to show that you do your most important business activities at home or that you do your administrative or management tasks at home. For example, if you are an interior decorator who works in clients' homes, you will qualify for the home office deduction if you do your planning, scheduling, billing, and so forth at home.

- **You meet clients or customers at home on a regular basis.** For example, if you are a masseuse who treats clients in your home or a couples' counselor who conducts therapy sessions at your home, you may take the home office deduction.

- **You use a separate freestanding structure on your property exclusively for business.** Some examples might be a detached garage, cottage, or workshop.

- **You store inventory or product samples at home.** However, you cannot have an outside office or other workplace outside your home. For example, if you are a traveling salesperson who goes to potential customers' homes to peddle your wares, you will qualify—unless you have an outside office for your business. You don't have to use your storage space exclusively for business to qualify—regular use is enough.

- **You run a day care center at home to care for children, people who are at least 65 years old, or those who are unable to care for themselves.** You don't have to use your day care space exclusively for business, but you must use it regularly. For example, if you use your living room for day care during the day and for entertaining and relaxing in the evening, you can still claim the deduction.

Your Home Office Might Be a Vehicle

You don't have to live and work in a house to take the home office deduction: Apartments, condominiums, or even motor homes, houseboats, and other vehicles that double as your home and workspace can qualify, but you must meet the tests set out above. The combined facts that you own a vehicle that you use as a residence and you run a business are not enough, in themselves, to prove your entitlement to the deduction.

Carlton Perry found this out the hard way, when the tax court disallowed all of his deductions for business use of his motor home. Perry claimed that he ran a real estate rental business from the vehicle, but couldn't show regular or exclusive use. The tax court was unmoved by the records he produced at trial: A 61-page handwritten account of the trips he and his wife took in the vehicle, which included entries on the flowers and trees they saw, the food they ate, the sunsets they watched, and the places they hiked together, but failed to make any mention of business use of the vehicle. (*Perry v. Commissioner of Internal Revenue*, TC Memo 1996-194.)

Don't expect the IRS to believe that you use most of a small home exclusively for your business, especially if you don't live alone. IRS auditors have homes, too, and they understand that it's very difficult to devote your only bedroom or all of your shared living space exclusively to your business.

For example, one taxpayer claimed that he used the "great room"—a combination living and dining room—of his rented house exclusively for his real estate business. The tax court didn't buy it, primarily because his home had only one bedroom and a kitchenette in addition to that great room, and his girlfriend lived with him. Although the court didn't doubt that he did some work at home, it refused to accept his argument that he and his girlfriend did all of their living, dining, and entertaining in the bedroom (or that the sofa and dining room table were used exclusively for work). (*Szasz v. Commissioner of Internal Revenue*, TC Summary Opinion 2004-169.)

USA TODAY Snapshots®

U.S. tax code multiplies

The basic publication explaining the tax code was 400 pages in 1913 when the income tax was established. Increase in pages:

1939 504
1969 16,500
1995 40,500
2009 70,320

Source: CCH Inc.

By Anne R. Carey and Alejandro Gonzalez, USA TODAY 2009

On the other hand, if you can prove that you really do use a lot of your living space for work, you might have a good claim. For example, a professional concert violinist successfully claimed the home office deduction for her entire living room, even though she shared a one-bedroom apartment with her husband and young daughter. The court noted that her living room contained no typical furnishings, only shelves for sheet music, recording equipment, a small table, and a chair for her practice sessions (and her daughter was not allowed to play there). (*Popov v. Commissioner of Internal Revenue*, 246 F.3d 1190 (9th Cir. 2001).)

What You Can Deduct

Using the home office deduction, you can deduct a portion of your household expenses, including:

- rent
- mortgage interest and property taxes (the advantage of taking a portion of these costs as a business deduction rather than a personal deduction—as you are entitled to do on IRS Schedule A, *Itemized Deductions*—is that it reduces your business income and so your self-employment taxes)
- condominium or homeowners' association fees
- depreciation on a home you own
- utilities
- insurance
- maintenance and cleaning
- security costs, and
- casualty losses.

The exact amount you can deduct depends on how much of your home you use for work. There are two ways to measure this:

- Using the room method, you divide the number of rooms you use for business by the total number of rooms in your home (not including bathrooms, closets, and other storage areas). For example, if you use the spare bedroom of your four-room home for business, you can deduct 25% of your household expenses.

- Under the square footage method, you divide the square footage of the area you use for work by the total square footage of your home (you don't have to include stairways, hallways, landings, entries, attics, or garages in your calculations). For example, if you use a 10' × 20' room as an office in your 1,000-square-foot home, your home office deduction percentage is 20%.

In addition to deducting a portion of overall household expenses, you may deduct 100% of any expense that is solely for your home office. For example, if you pay someone to paint the entire interior of your home (including your work area), you may deduct only the home office portion of the cost. But if you hire a painter just to paint your home office, you can deduct the entire amount.

Five Home Office Deduction Tips

Plenty of taxpayers don't take a home office deduction because they believe it is likely to trigger an audit. The IRS says such beliefs are misguided, but it never hurts to cover your bases. Follow these five tips to maximize your benefits—and minimize your chances of losing an audit.

Home Office Deduction Tip #1: Devote a Separate Room Exclusively to Your Side Business

While you can take a home office deduction even if you use only a portion of a room for work, it's much easier to designate an entire room: The math is easier, you won't have to worry about physically separating your work from your personal space, and you'll have an easier time satisfying the IRS that you use your office exclusively for work.

Home Office Deduction Tip #2: Do the Math to Figure Out Which Method Yields the Highest Deduction

Of course it's easier just to count rooms, but take the time to measure your square footage as well. Depending on your home's layout, it may give you a bigger deduction.

Home Office Deduction Tip #3: Create Visual Aids

Take a picture of your home office and draw up a simple diagram of your home layout showing the space you use for business. This can help you prove, if it's ever necessary, that you claimed the correct percentage.

Home Office Deduction Tip #4: Keep a Record of Home Office Activities and Save Receipts

If clients or customers visit, ask them to sign a log book. Note the time you spend on business in your date book or calendar. Save bills and receipts for home-office related expenses (like rent, utility payments, or house cleaning fees), along with your other business records.

Inventory Is Not a Business Expense

If you make or buy goods to sell, you may deduct the cost of those goods actually sold on your tax return. This is what you spent for the goods or their actual market value if they've declined in value since you bought them. However, this deduction is separate from the business expense deduction. Instead, you deduct the cost of goods you've sold from your business receipts to determine your gross profit from the business. Your business expenses are then deducted from your gross profit to determine your net profit, which is taxed. Businesses that make or buy goods to sell, must determine the value of their inventories at the beginning and the end of each tax year using an IRS-approved accounting method. Conducting inventories can be burdensome.

Home Office Deduction Tip #5: Use Your Home Office as Your Business Address

It will be easier to prove that your home is your principal place of business if you designate it as such. Have business mail delivered there and put your address on business correspondence, cards, and your letterhead.

For more information on inventories, see the Cost of Goods Sold section in Chapter 7 of IRS Publication 334, *Tax Guide for Small Businesses*; and IRS Publication 538, *Accounting Periods and Methods*; as well as Publication 970, *Application to Use LIFO Inventory Method*. You can obtain these and all other IRS publications by calling the IRS at 800-TAX-FORM, visiting your local IRS office, or downloading the publications from the IRS (www.irs.gov).

Deducting Long-Term Assets

Long-term assets are things that have a useful life of more than one year, as determined by the IRS. Examples include computers, equipment, machinery, and furniture. There are two ways to deduct long-term assets. You can:

- deduct them immediately under Section 179 of the Internal Revenue Code if they meet the requirements, or
- depreciate them (deduct a portion of the value each year of the item's useful life).

Special Rules for Computers, Cell Phones, and Other Potential Toys

The IRS has created special rules for things that can easily be used for personal purposes, including computers, vehicles, cell phones, stereo equipment, and cameras. For these types of property (called "listed" property), you are required to keep a log proving that you use the item for business, even if you use it only for business and never for fun. The only exception is computers: If you use your computer exclusively for business, you don't have to keep a log. The moral of the story, for many small-business owners, is that it makes more sense to buy a computer solely for business use than to go through the hassle of making a note every time you (or a family member) log on.

Immediate Deduction Using Section 179

Section 179 of the tax code allows you to deduct long-term assets in the year you buy them. You can't deduct more than you earn for the year, but you may carry over a Section 179 deduction to a future year, when your business is doing better. If you're fortunate enough to have skyrocketing profits, you can deduct up to a current limit of $250,000 (for tax year 2009). And in 2009, businesses that exceed the $250,000 deduction limit can take a bonus depreciation of 50% on the amount that exceeds the limit.

You can use Section 179 only for tangible personal property—in other words, you can't use it to deduct the cost of land or buildings, or intellectual property, such as patents and copyrights. To take the deduction, you must use the item more than half of the time for business in the year in which you buy it. This means that if you buy an item for personal use (such as a computer or desk), and then start using it in your business more than one year later, you can't use Section 179. It also means that if you use an item at least half of the time for personal (nonbusiness) purposes, you can't take the deduction. If you use the item more than half of the time for business, you may deduct only a percentage of what you paid—for example, if you paid $2,000 for a computer that you use 75% of the time for business, you can deduct $1,500.

Depreciation

Depreciation spreads your deduction out over the useful life of a long-term asset—three to seven years for most business equipment and electronics. Rather than deducting the entire cost at once, you take the deduction in installments, according to one of several formulas accepted by the IRS. Depreciation is pretty complicated; the IRS guide to the subject (Publication 946, *How to Depreciate Property*) is more than 100 pages long. There are exceptions, limits, and traps for unwary deduction claimers. If you're planning to use depreciation, get some accounting assistance.

Does Depreciation Ever Make Sense?

Unless your purchases of business property exceed the limit in a single year ($250,000 in tax year 2009), you'll probably be able to deduct long-term assets right away under Section 179. So why would anyone ever depreciate these assets instead?

Generally, people don't choose depreciation (unless they use the item less than half of the time for business, in which case they cannot use Section 179). In a couple of situations, however, spreading out your deductions makes sense:

- **You need to show a profit.** If you're pushing up against the IRS's hobby loss rule (discussed earlier in this chapter), you may need to show a profit in order to prove that you're really running a business. Depreciation gives you a smaller deduction, which might mean the difference between a profit and a loss.

- **You expect to earn more in the future.** If you expect to be in a higher tax bracket later, you might want to depreciate. Because the value of a tax deduction depends on your tax rate, a deduction will save you more in taxes if your earnings are higher.

Deducting Vehicle Expenses

Chances are that you do some driving for your side business—to pick up supplies, visit clients, go to the post office, and more. If you do, you can choose one of two ways to calculate your vehicle deduction: the standard mileage rate or the actual expense method.

- **Standard mileage rate.** This method allows you to claim a set deduction for every mile you drive for business (55 cents per mile for 2009; you can always find the current rate at www.irs.gov). You can claim a few additional expenses—including parking fees and tolls—on top of the mileage rate. You can't deduct the cost of

repairs, maintenance, gas, insurance, or other costs of operating
your car, because these costs are figured into the standard rate.
You can use the standard rate only for a car that you own. If you
don't use the standard rate in the first year when you drive your
car for business, you won't be able to use it for that car, ever.

- **Actual expense method.** Using this method, you deduct all of your
  car-related costs—including interest payments, insurance, license
  fees, oil and gas, repairs, and so on—for business use of your
  car. You can also depreciate the car, which means you take a set
  deduction each year to reflect the car's declining value over time.
  If you also use the car for personal reasons, you can deduct only
  a portion of your expenses. Using the actual expense method is
  much more time-consuming than using the standard mileage rate,
  but it might be worth the extra work if you have an expensive car,
  which will yield a fairly hefty depreciation deduction.

Whichever method you use, you'll have to keep careful records.
Because the IRS believes that taxpayers often overstate how much
they use their cars for business, it has some special rules for vehicle
deductions. You'll have to keep track of your business and personal
mileage; the easiest way to do this is to keep a log in your car and record
the odometer reading at the beginning and end of every business-related
drive. If you use the actual expense method, you'll also need to keep
records of all of your vehicle expenses.

Avoid the Commute by Working at Home

Ordinarily, you aren't allowed to deduct mileage for commuting—
driving between your home and your workplace. However, if you
qualify for the home office deduction, your home is your workplace. This means that you're logging deductible miles whenever
you leave home for business.

Deducting Travel Expenses

If you travel overnight for your side business, you can deduct your airfare, accommodations, and more. And the IRS doesn't require you to travel steerage; you can deduct your costs even if you stay at four-star hotels and enjoy the comforts of the first-class cabin.

However, the IRS also knows that most of us aren't going to travel to a distant city and spend our every waking moment working—we also want to see the sights. So it has created a set of rules delineating exactly which costs you can deduct and how much of your trip has to be business related in order to take a deduction. These rules depend on where you travel and how long you stay.

USA TODAY Snapshots®

Business travelers' pet peeves

What business travelers say is most annoying about being on the road:

Flight delays	51%
Being away from loved ones	33%
Not getting a restful sleep	30%
Airport security	27%

Note: Multiple responses allowed

Source: Braun Research for Embassy Suites Hotels online survey of 500 workers who took a business trip in 2008

By Anne R. Carey and Jeff Dionise, USA TODAY 2009

If you travel within the United States, your transportation costs (air and cab fare, for example) are deductible as long as you spend at least half of your trip on business. On days when you're doing business, you can also deduct your "destination" expenses, such as hotel costs, 50% of your meal expenses (see "Deducting Meals and Entertainment" for more on this 50% rule), local transportation (including car rental), telephone bills, and so on. On days when you're just having fun, you can't deduct these costs. And you can't deduct the cost of a spouse or other companion who comes along for the ride unless that person is your employee and has a genuine business reason for tagging along.

State Your Business

It isn't enough to keep records of what you paid for airfare, car rental, meals, and so on; you must also have some proof that you actually did business on your trip, in case you're audited. Take notes in your date book or calendar indicating whom you met with, sales calls, and other business activities. Keep copies of the business cards of people you spoke to, contracts you entered into, or other written records of the work you did.

If you don't collect and preserve this evidence, you could end up like Rick Richards, a screenplay writer and creator of country and gospel music, who tried to claim travel expenses for a number of trips he took with his wife. He claimed to have gone to Las Vegas, Nevada, and Branson, Missouri, to meet with performers and work on his screenplays. He also tried to deduct trips to Alaska and Mexico, including airfare, fare for a cruise ship, and the cost of escorted side tours, which he claimed to have taken to gather "on-site data and photos" for screenplay projects. (He also claimed all of his wife's expenses, because she went along as his photographer.) The court disallowed the expenses, finding that Richards couldn't prove that they were for business rather than pleasure. Although he kept records of what he paid for everything, none of those records indicated that the trips had a business purpose. (*Richards v. Commissioner of Internal Revenue*, TC Memo 1999-163.)

If you travel outside the United States, the rules depend on the length of your trip. If you're gone for fewer than seven days, you can deduct your transportation costs and your destination expenses for days you spend working. If your trip lasts more than seven days and you spend more than 75% of your time on business, the same rules apply. However, if you spend between 50% and 75% of your time on business, you may deduct only the business percentage of your transportation costs (you can still deduct destination costs for the days you spend working). And if you spend less than 50% of your time working, none of your costs are deductible.

Although these rules may already seem complicated, there are many more that are too detailed to explain here. The IRS has really gone to town in imposing requirements for travel deductions because this is an area where there has been a lot of abuse. As a result, they've written special rules for cruises, conventions, side trips, and more. For all the details, read IRS Publication 463, *Travel, Entertainment, Gift, and Car Expenses*.

Deducting Meals and Entertainment

If you entertain customers, advisers, suppliers, or other business associates, you may be able to deduct 50% of your costs. However, because lots of people have cheated on this deduction, there are many rules about what you can deduct and how you can prove that you really had a business purpose.

To claim a deduction, you must be with someone who can benefit your business in some way; you can't deduct the cost of entertaining family friends, for example, unless they also do business with you. In addition, you must actually discuss business before, during, or after the event. If you plan to claim that you discussed business during the event, you won't be able to deduct much more than meals, because the IRS believes that most types of entertainment—going to the theater, a ball game, or a cocktail lounge, for example—are not conducive to serious business discussions.

The IRS won't accept certain expenses as entertainment costs, including the cost of renting or buying an entertainment facility (such as a fishing lodge or tennis court), club dues, membership fees, or the cost of nonbusiness guests. This is another area where the rules can get pretty complicated. For more information, see IRS Publication 463, *Travel, Entertainment, Gift, and Car Expenses*.

My Big Fat Business Meeting Deduction

Discussing business at an event doesn't automatically make it a deductible entertainment expense. The IRS will look closely at the nature of the event—that is, whether it looks more like a business setting or a purely pleasurable one.

For example, one New Yorker tried to deduct part of the cost of his daughter's wedding reception as business entertainment. He claimed that 90 of the 242 guests were business associates or their spouses, that he spent exactly three-eighths of his total time speaking to them (including time in the receiving line), and that the conversations involved only business topics.

The court didn't buy this argument. Although it conceded that the taxpayer may have been seeking to improve business by inviting these guests to the wedding, it found that the reception was "a personal and family celebration"—not a business meeting. (*Leubert v. Commissioner of Internal Revenue*, TC Memo 1983-457.)

An Interview with Attorney Stephen Fishman

The following is an interview with attorney Stephen Fishman, who's the author of several of Nolo's books on tax deductions including *Deduct It! Lower Your Small Business Taxes*, *Home Business Tax Deductions*, *Every Landlord's Tax Deduction Guide*, and *Tax Deductions for Professionals*.

QUESTION: Steve, what's one tax deduction that a lot of people with side businesses overlook?

STEVE FISHMAN: One deduction many people don't take, even if they're entitled to it, is the home office deduction. Many people are afraid it will result in IRS audit, or they don't understand that they are entitled to it, and it is one of the best deductions for self-employed people.

If you use a home office exclusively for your business, you would be entitled to it, and it's especially a good deduction if you're a renter because it will enable you to deduct a portion of your rent, an expense that is ordinarily not deductible.

QUESTION: If you're making the home office deduction, which do you recommend using, the square footage method or the room method?

STEVE FISHMAN: I recommend trying both and using the one that gives you the greatest deduction. Generally, the room method will give you a larger deduction, but it won't always. It depends on how many rooms you have in your house. If you have one room, you'll be better off with the square footage. It depends on the size of the room and the number of square footage in your house. I would try both and use the one that gets the largest deduction.

QUESTION: You say in your books that you can't deduct commuting to your job, but that you can deduct traveling from your home office to a client. Why is that so?

STEVE FISHMAN: Commuting from home to the office or another workplace is considered a personal expense. Commuting from one business place to another is considered a business expense. When you have a home office, your home is now a place of business. So, you're going from one place of business to another. And that is now a business expense, not a personal expense.

QUESTION: Here's a similar question for travel deductions. Which makes more sense, using the standard mileage method or the actual expense method?

STEVE FISHMAN: The standard mileage method generally won't completely recompense you for your actual expenses, but it's much easier to use because there's far less record keeping involved. That's why most people use the standard mileage rate. If you like to get every cent you possibly can and you don't mind keeping track of every penny you spend on your car, you can use the actual expense method, and you will probably get a somewhat larger deduction. Of course, it depends how many business miles you drive.

QUESTION: The rules for deducting entertainment seem so tricky as to make it not worth the effort.

STEVE FISHMAN: It's not very hard at all. You just have to keep track of how much you spend and note the business reason for the expense, and keep your receipts. If they're more than $75, you get the deduction. For many people, it's an extremely valuable deduction—if you have a lot of business entertainment, you can deduct 50% of your business meals, which can be a very substantial deduction for some people. You have to have a business purpose—you have to eat with a client or a customer and you have to discuss business either before, during, or after the meal.

QUESTION: Steve, let's talk about the 179 deduction for a second. Because Congress has extended the amount that you can deduct under 179, does it ever make sense to claim depreciation?

STEVE FISHMAN: There are some things you can't use Section 179 for—for example, when you convert personal property to business property; and you can't use Section 179 for real property either. So there are times you have to use depreciation. If you spend over $500,000 in one year, your deduction is also limited under Section 179.

Also, if your income is quite low this year, you might prefer to depreciate the expense if you expect your income to go up substantially in future years. You take the depreciation deduction on those future years when your income is higher and you pay a higher tax rate.

QUESTION: What's a tax credit and how can you find out if your business is entitled to one?

STEVE FISHMAN: A tax credit is an amount you're allowed to deduct from your income tax. For example, if you get a $1,000 tax credit, you can deduct $1,000 from your income tax, which makes it much better than a tax deduction, which only reduces your taxable income. An example of a tax credit is when people refurbish their property to make it accessible for the disabled. You can have up to a $5,000 tax credit every year.

QUESTION: What kind of deductions can you make if your business is the victim of some natural catastrophe, such as an earthquake, a flood, or a hurricane?

STEVE FISHMAN: You may deduct the uninsured loss from your tax as a loss, a business loss.

QUESTION: What if the insurance hasn't paid? How do you know what you can deduct?

STEVE FISHMAN: You have to estimate how much you're likely to recover from your insurer and just deduct the amount that you don't expect to recover.

QUESTION: What kinds of deductions can a small-business owner make for retirement plans?

STEVE FISHMAN: Well, there are a vast array of deductions when you're self-employed. You have, of course, the traditional IRA, which anyone can have. You have special IRAs for self-employed people, called SEP IRAs.

QUESTION: When you say self-employed, do you mean you have your own business?

STEVE FISHMAN: That's right. You have your own business.

QUESTION: Because such a small percentage of people are audited, does a taxpayer really need to be that concerned about dotting their i's and crossing their t's when it comes to deductions?

STEVE FISHMAN: It really is true that only a small percentage of self-employed people are audited, only about 2%. So the odds are that you will not be audited. However, if you have a lot of odd-looking things on your tax return, that will definitely increase your chances of being audited. About 200,000 self-employed people were audited last year—there's always a chance you could be one of them. Depends if you want to play what they call "the audit lottery." You can do that and you may win. You may not. It's up to you. ●

Index

B

written agreements with, 177
See also Employees
Industry expertise, 214–215
Innovation, cultural drivers of, 126
Installation service business, 18–19
Insurance
  basic coverage, 97–102
  for employees, 103–105
  and home-based businesses, 167
  for liability issues, 96–97
  overview, 97, 98
  package deals, 102–103
  tips for saving money, 105–107
Insurance Information Institute, 102, 108
Insurance terms, 98
Insure.com, 108
Intellectual property audit (IP audit), 132–133
Intent-to-use application for trademark, 127
International sales, 82
Internet
  benefits of, 32–33
  driving traffic to your site, 44–48, 193
  free stuff, 33–37
  See also Websites
Internet connection, 159
Internet Service Providers (ISPs), 48
Invalidity provision of a contract, 119
Inventory
  insurance coverage for, 109
  slow turnover as cash flow problem, 62
  storing in a home office, 239
  tax deduction rules on, 237, 244
Investigating potential associates, 114–115
IRS
  audits, 214, 219–220, 231, 243–244, 255
  Cohan rule, 231

EIN form, 150–151, 178–179, 181
  on employees versus independent contractors, 175
  and employers' legal obligations, 177
  forms for independent contractor payments, 178–179
  and illegal earnings, 226
  penalty for misclassifying workers, 175
  record keeping for, 59, 229–232, 244
  standards for a business versus a hobby, 213–217
  taxation process, 220–222
  tax benefits of hiring your children, 184–185
  and unreported income, 229
  See also Tax deductions
IRS forms
  for C corporations, 91, 221
  for EIN, 150–151
  for employees, 179
  for independent contractor payments, 178–179
  for LLC members, 221
  overview, 222
  for partnerships, 221
  for S corporation shareholders, 221
  for self-employment taxes, 223
  for sole proprietorships, 220
  for unemployment taxes, 223
IRS publications
  on children as employees, 184
  on inventory, 244
  on record keeping, 59, 244
  on tax deductions, 230, 244, 246, 251
  tax guides, 61, 223, 234, 244

J

Janitorial business, 15
Jurisdiction provision of a contract, 117

T

Go to **Nolo.com/newsletters/index.html** to sign up for free newsletters and discounts on Nolo products.

- **Nolo Briefs.** Our monthly email newsletter with great deals and free information.

- **Nolo's Special Offer.** A monthly newsletter with the biggest Nolo discounts around.

- **BizBriefs.** Tips and discounts on Nolo products for business owners and managers.

- **Landlord's Quarterly.** Deals and free tips just for landlords and property managers, too.

 Don't forget to check for updates at **Nolo.com.** Under "Products," find this book and click "Legal Updates."

Let Us Hear From You

Comments on this book? We want to hear 'em. Email us at feedback@nolo.com.

US-SIDE1

NOLO® *Online Legal Forms*

Nolo offers a large library of legal solutions and forms, created by Nolo's in-house legal staff. These reliable documents can be prepared in minutes.

Online Legal Solutions

- **Incorporation.** Incorporate your business in any state.
- **LLC Formations.** Gain asset protection and pass-through tax status in any state.
- **Wills.** Nolo has helped people make over 2 million wills. Is it time to make or revise yours?
- **Living Trust (avoid probate).** Plan now to save your family the cost, delays, and hassle of probate.
- **Trademark.** Protect the name of your business or product.
- **Provisional Patent.** Preserve your rights under patent law and claim "patent pending" status.

Online Legal Forms

Nolo.com has hundreds of top quality legal forms available for download—bills of sale, promissory notes, nondisclosure agreements, LLC operating agreements, corporate minutes, commercial lease and sublease, motor vehicle bill of sale, consignment agreements and many, many more.

Review Your Documents

Many lawyers in Nolo's consumer-friendly lawyer directory will review Nolo documents for a very reasonable fee. Check their detailed profiles at **Nolo.com/lawyers/index.html**.

NOLO® Lawyer Directory

Find a Small Business Attorney

- *Qualified lawyers*
- *In-depth profiles*
- *Respectful service*

When you want help with your small business, you don't want just any lawyer—you want an expert in the field, who can provide up-to-the-minute advice to help you organize and run your enterprise so that you don't fall victim to legal pitfalls. You need a lawyer who has the experience and knowledge to answer your questions about protecting your personal assets, hiring and firing employees, drafting contracts, protecting your name and trademarks and a dozen other common business concerns.

Nolo's Lawyer Directory is unique because it provides an extensive profile of every lawyer. You'll learn about not only each lawyer's education, professional history, legal specialties, credentials and fees, but also about their philosophy of practicing law and how they like to work with clients. It's all crucial information when you're looking for someone to help you avoid as many legal problems as you can and solve the ones you can't.

All lawyers listed in Nolo's directory are in good standing with their state bar association. They all pledge to work diligently and respectfully with clients—communicating regularly, providing a written agreement about how legal matters will be handled, sending clear and detailed bills, and more. And many directory lawyers will review Nolo documents, such as a will or living trust, for a fixed fee, to help you get the advice you need.

WWW.NOLO.COM